Road Map to an American Renaissance

Road Map to an American Renaissance

John M. Humphrey

VANTAGE PRESS
New York

FIRST EDITION

Copyright © 1993 by John M. Humphrey

Published by Vantage Press, Inc.
516 West 34th Street, New York, New York 10001

Manufactured in the United States of America
ISBN: 0-533-10539-0

Library of Congress Catalog Card No.: 92-93442

0 9 8 7 6 5 4 3 2 1

Contents

List of Figures and Tables

Acknowledgments

I wish to acknowledge both the editorial and emotional support of my family and friends in the preparation of *Road Map to an American Renaissance*. The many philosophical threads of this work required more than the normal amount of editing to weave it into a presentable fabric. In particular, I want to thank my longtime friend, Miller Hudson, and my daughter, Diana Humphrey. Miller's considerable expertise in politics and government was of inestimable value in refining the many political positions and recommendations in this work. Diana's thorough review and verbal sensitivity was extremely valuable in removing rough spots in both the wording and the arguments.

Road Map to an American Renaissance

Prologue

I was motivated to write this book by twin convictions: (1) that the economic prosperity and political leadership of the United States of America are vitally important to the future prosperity of humanity, and (2) that America is failing to achieve the level of economic prosperity our great country is capable of. If this trend continues, we will eventually forfeit our position of political leadership as well.

The American spirit was forged by the challenges of the frontier and given direction by the eighteenth-century ideals of men of vision in both the Old and New Worlds. The spirit of self-reliance created by one hundred and fifty years of frontier living together with the relative isolation of the American colonies provided the necessary ingredients for a successful revolution against the feudal oppression of the Old World and for the creation of a society based on the ideals of human equality and freedom. For the past two hundred years, America has been both a beacon of political freedom and an engine of free enterprise economic prosperity.

The price of liberty is eternal vigilance. Throughout history, including our American history, mankind has sought to control others in order to prosper at their expense. Unfortunately, political control and the inevitable theft that follows, whether by force of arms or by legitimized systems, demotivates human effort and productive activity. As I view modern American society, I see a vast web of laws and regulations. While many of these laws are necessary in some form for our complex modern world, the extent of these laws is in the vast majority of cases excessive.

The vast array of governmental and commercial regulations

in modern American society exists primarily to serve special interests in our society who use these controls to prosper at our expense. Unfortunately, the pervasiveness of controls in our society means that most of us are both thieves and victims, often many times over. We vigorously defend the few controls that benefit us while at the same time only weakly opposing the hundreds of controls that individually usually only nickel and dime us.

This situation fosters a political system that spends vast resources promoting new schemes of legalized theft. These schemes are always presented as beneficial to the "general welfare" and they initially serve some useful purpose. Unfortunately, continuation of controls over a free market creates a dependent constituency that gradually institutionalizes the system. This process inevitably results in continually increasing costs for the desired benefit. Examples of this process range from the medical and legal professions on one end of the political spectrum to welfare, medicare, public housing, and a host of other government programs on the other end.

As we approach the twenty-first century we need a new American renaissance to reenergize both American prosperity and the American spirit. The new American renaissance will rekindle the torch of freedom to guide mankind's way into the next century. Like the old Renaissance, the new renaissance will require a climate of freedom that will promote prosperity through both hard work and innovation. The basic freedom—freedom from theft—motivates people both to work hard for today's prosperity and to innovate so we can all work smarter for tomorrow's prosperity.

My purpose in writing this book is to contribute to the restoration of American freedom, which I believe can lead to an American renaissance. I am not a political scientist, but the owner of a small Silicon Valley engineering company. My experiences with the feudal controls that inhibit American technology have served as the genesis of a much broader vision of the essential role of freedom in human society. I sincerely hope my observations and recommendations will spark creativity in the minds of readers so that together we can support the process of positive social innovation in America.

This book makes extensive use of categorization. For example, I define several categories for the types of theft in human society. Since the human experience is a continuum, events or situations will never fit perfectly into a finite number of categories. With this admission the reader is encouraged to view the use of categories, not as an absolute, but as simply a useful tool to promote understanding of important similarities and differences.

I chose the symbolism of a road map to provide a framework for discussing the journey of human prosperity. The two requirements of a road map are knowing where you are going and then deciding which road to take to get there. The first three sections of this book are devoted to achieving a better understanding of prosperity and the history of human systems that have fostered or inhibited prosperity. The fourth and fifth sections attempt to use these understandings to better evaluate some of the controls that are currently inhibiting American prosperity and then present some recommendations. Every road follows many twists and turns in reaching its destination. While I encourage the reader to critically examine each turn, I humbly request the reader to try to view these turns in the overall context of the journey.

1 / The Search for Prosperity

Life's Eternal Search for Prosperity

The evolution of life on earth (and presumably throughout the universe) is driven by the objective of survival. For evolutionary purposes, survival is really a continuous spectrum better described by words like *more successful* and *prosperous*. While an individual organism may live or die, depending on how well it copes with a given situation, random variations in conditions make survival of a species a statistical process based on probability. Therefore, natural selection keeps acting to make each species more successful or prosperous so that a greater percentage of the members survive. This understanding of prosperity as the goal of natural selection is essential to understanding human behavior.

The level of prosperity is determined by just two parameters: ability and motivation. Some people would add luck as a third parameter. However, luck is a random variable that normalizes out over time. Ability is the measure of how efficiently we can accomplish a task to obtain resources (i.e., how smartly we can work). Today's ability is the result of yesterday's education, investment, and innovation; for example, our individual ability is determined by our natural ability (past biological innovations), our past education, and the tools we own (past investment). While our ability determines how efficiently we can work, our motivation determines how hard we work to obtain resources. Together these two factors— how hard we work and how efficiently we work—determine our level of prosperity.

5

Future growth in prosperity requires improvements in ability. The hours of the day limit how hard we can work, but there is no limit as to how efficiently we can work. The three ways to improve ability are education, investment, and innovation. Education is the process of training the mind and body to more efficiently perform certain tasks. Investment is the creation of tools that augment our ability in performing tasks more efficiently. Finally, innovation is the discovery of new ways to perform tasks more efficiently.

Each of the three ability enhancements has a service life. Education only lasts for the lifetime of the individual. Each new generation must relearn the skills of their parents. Investment can have a longer lifetime, but it too depreciates and must be continually renewed. Innovation is forever. Of the three ability enhancements, only innovation is permanent. Knowledge can be lost, but it does not depreciate. Each new generation must learn arithmetic, but the priceless innovation of Arabic numbers does not have to be reinvented. The permanence of innovation makes it the only way to achieve enhanced long-term prosperity. The evolution of life on earth is a record of the successful and unsuccessful innovations that have been evaluated to achieve enhanced prosperity.

There are three categories of innovation: The first is biological innovation, which is the more efficient arrangement of cells to form an organism. This also includes instinct, which is hard wiring the brain to achieve permanent education. The second is social innovation, which is the more efficient arrangement of social units of biological organisms (examples include herd behavior among prey, pack-hunting behavior among predators, and schools, marriage, the rule of law, etc., among human beings). The third is technical innovation, which is the discovery of knowledge that enables us to more efficiently interact with the environment, usually by building more efficient tools.

The Paradox of Order and Disorder

Paradoxically, the survival and prosperity of life require both order and disorder. Order provides both motivation and direction to efficiently use ability to the best advantage to produce today's prosperity. Disorder provides the conditions that foster innovations needed to enhance ability for tomorrow's prosperity. Devising a system that both provides order and fosters innovation through disorder is one of the most fundamental challenges of life.

Biological organisms meet the requirements for order and innovation sequentially. The lifetime of the organism is based on order, with no genetic modifications permitted. If a group of cells should decide to grow a third arm or a big tumor, the organism has no way of determining whether or not this mutation would be beneficial. Therefore, living organisms do not permit biological innovation, and they ruthlessly crush any mutations that arise. Biological innovations that are essential for long-term adaptability and prosperity only occur between generations. Therefore, the biological cycle of life, reproduction, and death is nature's solution to achieving both order and innovation. The length of time between generations represents a trade-off between biological complexity and rapid biological adaptability in the race for prosperity.

Development of the higher levels of the brain was a giant evolutionary leap for both order and innovation. The higher levels of the brain provided the capability to become educated by remembering the experiences of life and then by developing learned behaviors to more efficiently respond to the natural environment. Without the capability for education, all the information required to build and operate an organism had to be encoded in the DNA and inefficiently replicated in each and every cell. While the DNA is truly a marvelous biological innovation, DNA alone is not capable of defining both the structural architecture and the increasingly complex behavioral patterns of complex organisms. The expansion of the brain provided an extra DNA reservoir for instructions, particularly behavioral instructions. Although research indicates that information may be redundantly stored in the brain, this is still far more efficient than storing the information in each cell. The expansion of the brain dramatically increased the ability of life to prosper by learning complex behaviors that would have been impossible to program into the DNA. The obvious disadvantage of extra DNA information storage is the requirement for education to teach each new generation the skills of their parents.

The capability for education made possible by an enlarged brain provided the ability to innovate by adapting behavior to the current conditions in an animal's lifetime. This ability to be behaviorally programmed (i.e., educated) significantly reduced the time constant for adaptation. Rather than biologically adapt through random genetic mutations, which are fixed for the life of the organism, education permitted an organism to learn by trying different behaviors and then adopting those that proved most successful. Although higher animals retained instinctive behaviors, they were able to modify these behaviors through education to accommodate changing conditions. The adaptability provided by education enabled nature to favor development of increasingly complex organisms that could retain the ability to innovate.

The ability of education to enhance both order and innovation has been a central focus in mankind's social development. Human social groups achieve enhanced ability through both shared experience and specialization. Shared experience enables many to more efficiently gain knowledge from the experiences of one member of the group. Specialization allows the group to increase their collective ability by allowing each member to concentrate his education in a different area. Both these methods also enhance innovation. Specialization increases each member's ability to develop social or technical innovations in his area of expertise, and shared experience makes these innovations available to the entire group.

While many aspects of education function to support both order and innovation, the strong age preference of education brings these two requirements for prosperity into conflict. While education can be received throughout an organism's lifetime, the receptiveness to education is much greater in the young. Current research indicates that the process of education in the young results in actual physical changes to the brain as it becomes hard wired based on accumulated experience. For example, although a person can learn a foreign language later in life, he can never achieve the fluency of a native speaker. This process may be something like the action of a computer compiler, which converts higher level computer codes to machine language. The ability to convert behaviors to "machine language" apparently ends at puberty when the structure of the brain becomes fixed. The maturation of the brain provides each generation the opportunity to obtain a more contemporary understanding of the world than their parents. When each new generation reaches adulthood, they have the opportunity to use the understandings they have received through education to develop social and technical innovations to enhance prosperity.

Mankind's age-limited ability to receive education is a form of biological damping on the process of innovation. In the same way that organisms oppose biological innovation during their lifetimes, so the "generation gap" phenomena in human education leads people to oppose social and technical innovations in their lifetime. This process ensures a more orderly society by delaying social changes until the generation that was educated to the need for a social or technical change gains control of the society. However, the generation gap effect can also threaten prosperity when conditions change rapidly and a society is unable to respond to those changes. Fortunately the mature human mind is also able to receive education to a remarkable degree. This ability mitigates the generation gap effect and enables properly structured societies to efficiently respond to change.

Throughout history rigid social structures that thwart innovation have posed one of the greatest threats to human prosperity. These institutions function like immortal biological organisms that perceive innovation as a threat to their existence. Like the biological organisms they mimic, the real threat to their existence is their failure to respond to the inevitable need to adapt and improve. Innovation is their opportunity to prosper and avoid extinction. However, permitting some disorder (and potential loss of prosperity) today, to ensure survival and prosperity tomorrow, is too enlightened a concept for many of these institutions. They tenaciously hold on to existing behaviors and methods until the inevitable forces of change lead to their extinction. The collapse of communism around the world is an example of this process. Communism was born in response to glaring deficiencies in the operation of free enterprise capitalism. However, capitalism continued to positively evolve through the forces of democratic change while communism did not evolve and therefore became extinct.

Modern American society has many entrenched institutions that thwart innovation and thereby reduce American prosperity. One of the great challenges to an American renaissance will be to identify these roadblocks to prosperity and pursue democratic methods to remove them with minimum disruption to American society.

Predation and Human Freedom

Predation is an essential feature of the survival and prosperity of life. The second law of thermodynamics says that the disorder of all closed systems increases with time. Therefore growth which is essential to survival and prosperity requires an infusion of energy from outside the system. With the exception of a few geothermal ecosystems, the sun is the energy source for all life on Earth. While the sun consumes itself in the process of fusion, its radiation provides a net source of energy for life on earth.

Solar radiation and natural elements were the only inputs for early life on earth. Photosynthesis allowed life to liberate carbon from carbon dioxide for organic molecules. The resulting free

10

oxygen provided a chemical energy source when the sun was not shining. The predation of life on natural elements, sunlight, and the free oxygen released by photosynthesis led to the evolution of increasingly complex species of plants.

The presence of free oxygen that permitted oxidation of a cell's own matter when the sun was not shining also permitted oxidation of any other available organic matter. This situation presumably led to cells that increasingly fed on other cells rather than photosynthesize food themselves. The biological innovation of plant predation led to the evolution of herbivorous animals. The existence of herbivorous animals led to the biological innovation of carnivorous animals and omnivorous animals with a proliferation of animal species, including quite recently our own.

Predation is one of nature's finest tools for fostering innovation through the mechanism of survival of the fittest. From the aerobatic ability of flying fish to the stripes of the tiger, nature favors innovations that enhance survival and nature eliminates through extinction those innovations that do not. The predator/prey relationship is both a more critical and a more discriminating judge of strength and stamina than the natural elements alone.

Predator and prey species have developed symbiotic social relationships that make predation an even more effective tool of natural selection. Herd behavior in land animals and schooling behavior in fish act to selectively screen both the weakest prey and the weakest predators. Without herd behavior, the fleetest prey and the fastest predators would still have a statistical advantage. However, random encounters could occasionally result in a sickly lion killing a fleet antelope. The mechanism of herd flight selectively moves the fittest prey to the front of the herd and the slowest prey to the rear where they fall victim to the fastest predators. Therefore nature favors methods of predation that enhance fitness in species and rewards these successful biological innovations.

Throughout the evolution of life, predation within animal species has been discouraged. Each species seeks to fill a biological

11

niche based on successful predation on certain other species of plants and/or animals and successfully avoiding becoming the prey of other animal species. Survival depends on each species's ability to successfully compete for a limited supply of resources. Whereas predation culls the weakest members of a species, self-predation frequently kills the strongest. In a close race for survival, the resulting debasement of the gene pool can easily lead to the extinction of a species.

Mating contests are an example of nature's avoidance of self-predation. These contests to determine the strongest or fittest males for breeding are another powerful tool of natural selection. While these mating contests must be sufficiently violent to establish the physically superior suitor, they generally stop short of death or even serious injury. Fatal contests between the strongest males would remove the fittest individuals and be detrimental to the survival of the species.

Self-predation is one of the most distinguishing behavior characteristics of our species. Since this book seeks to promote human liberty as the best prosperity-enhancing strategy for mankind, we face the awesome intellectual challenge of understanding both the detrimental and the positive effects of self-predation in human history. My purpose here is not in any way to demean the noble ideals of the God-given inalienable rights of man that are the moral foundation of America. Instead I seek to strengthen that foundation through an objective understanding of the advantages of human liberty. Nature favors those systems that work best to promote the survival and ultimate prosperity of a species. With two hundred years of American history under our belt, we are in a strong position to defend liberty because it works, not just because it seems morally right.

The prosperity of the United States (both in economic terms and also in human values made possible by economic prosperity) contrasted against the extinction of competing systems based on tyranny provides compelling experimental evidence that freedom works. However, these data do not explain why freedom enhances prosperity or how civilization was able to progress so far under predatory social and political systems. The rest of this chapter is devoted to an overview of the evolution and effects of human self-predation.

Human self-predation likely had its roots as a form of breeding dominance behavior. Mankind evolved as a relatively small animal that required the strength of an extended family for survival. As with many other species, competition for the best territory is an important element of survival. When food becomes scarce, the human families that were able to claim or hold the best territory were more likely to survive and prosper. We are not the only species to defend territory to promote survival, but we are clearly the only species to use territorial dominance on such a large scale, first through extended families, then as tribes, and now as nations.

Several thousand years ago, we became the first species to achieve a level of civilization based on social and technical innovation where most of the resources that we needed to prosper were the output of efforts by our own species. We used technology to accumulate wealth, first in the form of stored food or herds of livestock and then later in the form of houses, clothes, and a host of manufactured goods. This situation gave mankind two paths to prosperity: produce the resources we needed using our own efforts assisted by other species and the natural environment (i.e., work for a living), or prey on (steal from) our fellowman.

The principal benefit of self-predation in human society has been the opportunity and motivation for innovation. By releasing certain more able individuals from the daily chore of survival, human self-predation enabled those individuals to develop both social and technical innovations that enhanced the prosperity of the entire society. The creation of social structures, the development of written language, and the knowledge of agriculture together with a calendar to guide planting are examples of the many early innovations that flowed from a leisure (i.e., ruling) class of nobles and priests. As civilization advanced, the use of warfare enabled entire nations to become affluent through predation on others. The flowering of culture and technology in Egypt, Greece, Rome, and all the other great civilizations of the ancient world was made possible by the leisure time obtained through successful human self-predation.

The paradoxical rise of civilization in the face of continual warfare has been due to the strong positive feedback between war and the advance of technology through technical innovation. The development of technology through technical innovation is often an expensive and time-consuming effort. In ordinary life, any investment in ability (including innovation, education, and capital investment) to enhance future prosperity reduces the resources available for consumption to support today's prosperity. Mankind's time value of money, which economists tell us is about 3 percent plus inflation, limits investment to those projects that exceed this payout.

However, the narrow margin of victory in war together with the severe penalties for defeat provide strong incentives for developing advanced technology. Therefore throughout human history, the prodigious cost of armaments and the frightful cost of their use in wars to support mankind's self-predation have resulted in a much more rapid advance in technology than would otherwise have occurred. After the war, the technology developed for war can be applied commercially to improve the standard of living with relatively little additional cost. The development of metallurgy in the ancient world (i.e., from swords to plowshares) and the development of the airplane in modern times are two such examples. Clearly this technology could have been developed at far less cost without war; but without the threat (or incentive of war), the resources would have been spent on current consumption with no benefit to future prosperity.

The principal disadvantages of self-predation in human society have been the high cost to current prosperity required to enforce self-predation and the high cost to future prosperity resulting from the demotivating effects of self-predation on the victims. Human societies have developed a wide variety of mechanisms to reduce these negative effects and thereby improve the cost/benefit ratio of human self-predation. The cost of warfare was mitigated by the development of stable empires that allowed conquered peoples to live in peace in return for payment of tribute in the form of wealth or slaves. The empire also provided security in the form of military protection from other empires. While the subsequent development of colonies was a more benign form of imperialism, the basic purpose was still to achieve prosperity for the mother country through predation. Within societies, the development of hereditary class structures or religious castes institutionalized theft in an attempt to reduce both the cost of stealing current wealth and the demotivating effect of this theft on the production of future wealth.

The intellectual foundation for liberty as a superior prosperity-enhancing strategy for mankind rests on both the decline of the advantages of human self-predation and the significant increase in its cost. Prosperity is best enhanced by maximizing the productive capabilities of the entire population. In a subsistence culture, predation permitted a few hopefully more able individuals to devote at least some of their time to improving the ability of the civilization through education and then innovation. Their predation did not deprive others of this opportunity, because there wasn't enough wealth to raise the entire population above a subsistence level.

Unfortunately as civilization advanced, an increasing share of the proceeds of self-predation were spent on pretentious consumption. The decadence of the later Roman Empire is an historical example. This phenomenon of excess wealth acting to reduce innovative output among the wealthy few is important. Of far greater significance, the concentration of excess wealth and power in the hands of a few individuals deprived the majority of the opportunity to become educated and to contribute to the innovative process. These two effects—the decreased productivity of the idle rich and the unrealized talent of the rest of the society—strongly favor a system that allows each individual the freedom to maximize his ability for the prosperity of the society.

The increasingly nonproductive use of wealth by the ruling classes in society was mirrored by a dramatic increase in the cost of predation. Advances in military technology increased the cost of war to such an extent that military contests among near equals were no longer a net benefit to the victor. As living standards continued to increase, the benefits of predation were further reduced by the increasing impact of victim demotivation. The failure of communism around the world is a powerful example of the failure of predation due to demotivation of the workers. When the size of the pie shrinks because the bakers are not motivated to work, cutting a larger slice still leaves the predators with a small piece.

Human liberty is an engine for prosperity in the modern world because freedom motivates each individual to be productive for today's prosperity and to enhance his ability for tomorrow's prosperity. The standard of living is high enough today that predation no longer benefits society and the costs of predation have become unacceptable. However, liberty faces two significant challenges in the modern world. First, the price of liberty is eternal vigilance because mankind will always be tempted to steal whenever the cost/benefit ratio is attractive. The prevalence of both legalized and illegal theft in modern American society is a formidable threat to our future prosperity.

Second, the strong present-mindedness of our species directs too little resources to future investment. The old saying that "necessity is the mother of invention" should be expanded to "necessity is a powerful incentive for all forms of ability improvement." The threat of predation during the cold war has been a very effective incentive for education, investment, and of course for technical innovation. Mankind needs to replace the threat of military confrontation with peaceful competition to maintain a balance between current consumption for today's prosperity and investment in ability for future prosperity.

2 / The Evolution of Prosperity

The Evolution of Living Power Structures

The evolution of life to achieve prosperity has been accomplished through increasingly more efficient arrangements of living tissue. During the early stage of evolution, this process focused on improvements in the structure of single-celled organisms. While this process continued, the primary path of evolution has been the arrangement of cells into living power structures (PS). These collections of cells working together could accomplish tasks that would be impossible for single-celled organisms and thereby enhance the survivability and prosperity of the group.

The evolution of living power structures has proceeded through four stages, with mankind presently struggling to fully achieve the fourth stage. These four stages are summarized in the table opposite and the following paragraphs.

The four stages in the evolution of living power structures are differentiated both by the ways in which living cells combine and by the power structures that are their source of competition.

Biological power structures are what we normally think of when we think of evolution. Through the process of biological innovation, living cells banded together to form organisms that could work more efficiently. Initially these organisms were just colonies of cells, but gradually through the process of specialization the individual cells gave up their separate identities and became part of a common organism, or biological power structure. Each

THE FOUR STAGES OF LIVING POWER STRUCTURES (PS)

STAGE	DESCRIPTION	COMPETITION FOR SURVIVAL
1) BIOLOGICAL	COLLECTION OF INDIVIDUAL CELLS	ALL OTHER BIOLOGICAL POWER STRUCTURES
2) SOCIAL	COLLECTION OF BIOLOGICAL PS OF THE SAME SPECIES	BIOLOGICAL PS OF OTHER SPECIES
3) POLITICAL	COLLECTION OF BIOLOGICAL PS OF THE SAME SPECIES	BIOLOGICAL PS OF THE SAME SPECIES
4) ENLIGHTENED	COLLECTION OF BIOLOGICAL PS OF THE SAME SPECIES	ALL OTHER PS WITH RETURN BASED ON PRODUCTION (I.E., THEFTLESS COMPETITION)

TABLE 2–1

biological organism is in competition with every other organism for survival.

Social power structures are associations of biological power structures that cooperate to enhance their survival. These associations can be rigid, as among social insects, or relatively loose. However, the common thread of socialization is a reduction in competition and conflict within a group or species and a more focused competition against other species.

Political power structures are a refinement of social power structures whereby biological power structures form associations to compete against similar associations of their own species. Political power structures typically operate within social power structures to enhance the prosperity of a smaller group of biological power structures. The greater efficiency of political associations can be directed entirely at enhanced productive effort. More typically, political associations are directed in part at self-predation, or theft, from members of their own species.

Enlightened power structures are associations of biological power structures that band together to enhance their prosperity through theftless competition. Enlightened power structures are guided by the understanding that self-predation diminishes the prosperity of the species. If self-predation (theft) merely shifted wealth from one group to another, there would be no net effect on overall prosperity. However, theft demotivates both the thief and the victim from performing productive effort. Therefore, theft results in a net loss of wealth to the species. In contrast, the freedom that exists within enlightened power structures encourages each individual to prosper and thereby promotes the prosperity of the group.

The next four sections provide a more detailed discussion of each of the four stages of living power structures. When viewed as a common framework, this discussion unifies the separate threads of biological, social, and political development. The search of living power structures for prosperity is achieved through innovation, production of wealth, theft, and ultimately freedom. The insights from this unified approach will be used to gain further understanding of human history and to help formulate recommendations for our American renaissance.

Biological Power Structures

Biological power structures are the first stage in the evolution of living power structures. Through the biologically innovative processes of genetic mutation and natural selection, single cells banded together to form organisms which were better able to survive and prosper. These biological power structures had several important characteristics that are worth examining, because they

19

have parallels in the more advanced stages of living power structures.

Altruism is the most fundamental characteristic of all biological power structures. The individual cells, which all share the same DNA, cease to compete with each other and instead direct their efforts toward enhancing the survival of the organism. Cells that lose this altruistic orientation or deviate in any way from their common genetic program are called "cancerous" and are destroyed to preserve the organism.

Specialization is one of the more important advantages of a multicelled organism. Through the process of specialization, cells banded together to form organs within the organism specifically adapted to perform selected functions more efficiently and on the larger scale required to support the needs of the organism. Sensory organs evolved to provide input on the surrounding environment. digestive and circulatory systems evolved to provide food and oxygen and remove waste products. Muscles and bones evolved to permit movement; and lastly, a brain and nervous system evolved to direct and coordinate action.

All higher forms of life on earth have adopted a centralized authoritarian command and control system. A centralized brain makes decisions based on sensory input, and these decisions are followed without question by the other cells of the organism.

The degree of redundancy is a fundamental decision for all multicelled organisms. The disadvantage of specialization is that individual cells are no longer self-sufficient. Therefore, failure of a key function through injury or disease can doom the entire organism. Organisms achieve redundancy either by overcapacity (e.g., an oversized liver) or by multiple organs (e.g., two arms, two eyes, two kidneys, etc.). Also, organisms have the ability to regenerate damaged tissue to varying degrees. Since redundancy tends to compromise some of the advantages of specialization, the degree of redundancy is minimized.

Size is another fundamental decision for all organisms. Biological survival includes the twin objectives of environmental adaptability and competition with other biological power structures within the food chain. Smaller organisms are more adaptable because they respond faster to random genetic mutations. Smaller organisms are also better able to adjust to changes in the environment or to recover their numbers after some environmental disaster. However, size gives larger organisms advantages either as a predator or in the ability to avoid becoming prey, or both. The process of natural selection leads to a spectrum of species of varying sizes. More stable climates such as occurred during the age of the dinosaurs favor the evolution of larger organisms that are more susceptible to mass extinctions when there are severe changes in the environment.

Social Power Structures

An understanding of social power structures is fundamental to the understanding of biological evolution, because the evolution of biological and social power structures are intimately related. Social power structures are associations of biological power structures that cooperate to enhance their competition for survival against other species. The study of ants, for example, requires both an understanding of the biology of the individual ant and an understanding of the social dynamics of the ant nest. In the same way that individual cells behave selflessly in the interest of the organism they are a part of, so individual ants behave selflessly in the interest of the nest. In the same way that individual cells specialize in a biological power structure, individual ants specialize as workers, soldiers, etc., to enhance the collective survival of the ant nest. In the same way that the brain controls an organism, so the ant queen controls the ant nest. In the same way that biological organisms do not permit genetic innovation, so ant colonies destroy any mutations that arise. In a very real sense, the ant nest is an organism that is both capable of achieving tasks beyond the capabilities of its individual members, yet is more flexible than a single biological organism of equivalent mass. In hard times, the nest can shrink to accommodate available food supplies and then rapidly rebuild when conditions improve.

While insects have developed the closest integration between their social and biological structures, many other species have highly developed social structures. Herd behavior is very common among prey species. Herd behavior enhances the survival of the prey species by allowing the strongest males to control the reproductive process. As discussed earlier, herd flight is a natural discriminator that separates the strong and healthy animals at the front of the herd from the old and weak individuals that drift toward the rear and fall victim to the predators. Therefore, herd behavior in land animals and schooling behavior in fish serves to enhance the survival of the prey species by promoting the survival of the fittest individuals.

Social behavior is common but not universal in predator species. Predators need to be fast enough and big enough to capture prey. Bengal tigers who live in densely vegetated areas with relatively stable climates have chosen large size and camouflage rather than social development as their path to prosperity. Wolves, on the other hand, evolved pack hunting behavior, which permits them to prey on larger animals while keeping the size of the individual wolf relatively small in response to their harsh environment and uncertain food supply. Coyotes and foxes have chosen the tiger's approach of solitary hunting and larger size relative to their prey. Our cousins the baboons have evolved a well-developed social structure that enhances their survival against predators and provides for improved care and education of their young.

Humanity is an important example of the interaction of biological and social evolution. While little is known of the social structure of early man, the baboon model of closely knit tribes seems most reasonable. The development of hands allowed us to

22

develop tools; but just as important, hands allowed us to do things for each other. Old men could make flint arrowheads for younger men to use in hunting. Old women could make clothes for others to use. Protecting the old and weak from predators was now in the common interest. As technology improved, the advantage of occupational specialization increased. But unlike ants whose only specialization is based on biological differences, our specialization was based both on biological differences and on education. The advantages of specialization through education favored large brains with improved mental abilities. However, more complex social and occupational structures made possible by larger brains required longer periods of apprenticeship. Our biology accommodated this need with a long period of adolescence, which was now possible due to the social support of the extended family. Our long period of adolescence led to increased occupational specialization between males and females, with the males concentrating on spacial abilities (e.g., spear throwing) and the females concentrating on relationship skills and later on verbal abilities.

The development of language was a profound sociobiological innovation. Language, at least initially, is of little value to a solitary creature; but spoken language and later written language significantly improved humanity's ability to form successful social power structures. Language greatly enhanced the ability for shared experience and for the orderly direction of group undertakings. Language permitted abstract reasoning and generalizations that are essential to higher thought processes. These higher thought processes combined with shared experience dramatically increased the rate of human social and technical innovation. Use of language required the biological evolution of human vocal cords and specialized brain structures to control them. The use of language led to increasingly more complex human social structures that favored increased brain development to cope with these social complexities.

The combined biological and social development of mankind led us to become the dominant species on our planet by about the end of the last Ice Age. While an individual man was no match for a mammoth, the Neolithic tribes that invaded the Americas during the last Ice Age drove the mammoth and many other species of large animals to extinction. I believe this event and similar events around the world were significant because anthropologists tell us that there has been very little biological evolution in our species since we achieved this position of dominance about twenty thousand years ago. This experience suggests that once a species achieves dominance, the removal of external competition causes natural selection to operate on the social structure as a whole. This tends to stall biological innovation by thwarting the natural selection process that would otherwise more strongly discriminate among the individual members of the group.

The social structures of higher animals are different from the social structures of social insects in two important respects. First, while the higher animals who join social structures are of the same species and therefore genetically similar, they are not biologically identical. Second, the process of specialization by education leads to behaviors that are not commonly shared by the other members of the social group. In contrast, groups of social insects share both a common heredity and common behaviors because all physical and behavioral characteristics are programmed in their DNA.

Lack of either a completely common heredity or completely common behaviors in the social power structures of higher animals weakens the bond of altruism that is a fundamental requirement for any living power structure. This reduced sense of altruism creates a command and control crisis in the social power structure. All biological power structures operate based on an absolute centralized command structure with unquestioning obedience from all other cells of the organism. Cellular obedience is voluntary and uncoerced, because all cells share a common heredity and therefore a completely common purpose. The lack of common purpose within the social power structures of higher animals means that individual members of the group are tempted to act contrary to the best interests of the group when such actions significantly enhance their own prosperity. These natural selfish motivations ("original sin") are the basis of all antisocial behaviors in the social power structures of high animals, including man.

Political Power Structures

Political power structures are the direct result of the lack of common purpose within the social power structures of higher animals. The lack of complete altruism in these social power structures undermines the group's command and control structure and tempts individual members to pursue their own self-interest. Political power structures formed as social power structure subgroups with greater common interest. This greater common interest gave political power structures a stronger sense of altruism toward the members of their subgroup and therefore a more efficient command and control structure.

The purpose of political power structures is to enhance the prosperity of a group of individuals relative to other members of the same species. Political power structures can contribute to the prosperity of the larger social group through specialization and their greater ability to organize their efforts. In this mode, political power structures behave like organs of the body efficiently performing some function. However, political power structures can also become predators on the social group. In this mode, they are analogous to a cancer. Most political power structures exhibit both these characteristics.

The greatest challenge for social power structures is to continually monitor and direct the self-interest of their political power structures along lines that will benefit the society as a whole. The primary mechanism for restraining antisocial behavior is through the establishment of rules that define the limits of socially acceptable behavior. Political power structures are permitted to pursue their own self-interest as long as they play by these agreed upon "rules of the game." Since the rule of law is the essential fabric that preserves social unity, it provides the most powerful tool for political theft. For example, the perniciousness of AIDS results from the corruption of the body's immune system, which is the very structure we depend on for defense against infection. In the same way, the perniciousness of legalized theft results from the corruption of the rule of law, which is the mechanism that we depend on to preserve social unity by defining mutually beneficial social behaviors.

Redundancy is another effective social mechanism for curbing antisocial behavior by political power structures. Redundancy in biological power structures serves to limit the vulnerability of the organism to the loss of a vital specialized function. We have two physically separate kidneys so that we can maintain this vital function even with the loss of one kidney through injury or disease. Redundancy of key political power structure functions in society (e.g., two companies making electric light bulbs or polio vaccine) serves the biological function of ensuring the availability of vital functions. However, redundancy in social power structures also provides for competition and innovation.

Competition is not necessary in biological power structures because altruism keeps all the cells of the body working for the common good. In society, competition between political power structures performing redundant functions keeps each political power structure focused on meeting society's needs and thereby thwarts excessive self-directed cancerous tendencies. Competition is also a powerful incentive for innovation, which increases social prosperity through more efficient use of resources. The ability of political power structures under the stimulus of competition to innovate for their own prosperity and ultimately for society's prosperity is an important evolutionary advancement.

The evolutionary emphasis on political power structures in human civilization was driven by the two factors of technology and wealth. Technology can be broadly defined as the ability to create the resources needed for survival and prosperity. In this sense, ants possess technology through their ability to construct complicated nests that protect them from predators and the environment, store food, provide a nursery for their young, and in general enhance their survival potential. The existence of technology makes a social power structure both less dependent on predation on other species for prosperity and more tempted toward self-predation. I understand that there is even a species of ants that captures and enslaves other ants. The slave ants build tunnels, care for the young, and perform the many other tasks required to keep their captors' nest running. By comparison, lions are the dominant species on the plains of Africa through their well-developed social power structure. However, they must still hunt for food (i.e., they have no technology); and therefore, they have no incentive to enslave other groups of lions. Similarly, Ice Age man was also a hunter with limited technology. Although he became the dominant species on earth through his well-developed social power structure, he had little incentive to try to control other groups of men.

The accumulation of wealth made possible by the advance of technology created a compelling incentive for the development of human political power structures whose prosperity was based on self-predation. Although our biological evolution stalled about twenty thousand years ago, the prosperity of our species increased rapidly through significant social and technical innovations. Mankind learned to cultivate crops, especially grains, as a more secure and efficient source of food; domesticate animals for food, clothing, transportation, companionship, and heavy work; and to use the forests for building materials and to farm the sea for food. As mankind became increasingly prosperous, we began to accumulate wealth in the form of stored food, herds of domesticated animals, tools, clothes, and structures. This wealth was a source of future prosperity both for those who created it and for anyone with the ability to take it by theft.

A broader understanding of theft is necessary to understand

human political control. Stripped of its moral frameworks, theft is really the word we use to describe human self-predation. Theft is simply the transfer of resources between human beings at less than free-market value. In this book, the term "free market" means an uncoerced exchange of resources. This is a more limited definition than the unrestrained behavior sometimes used by economists to describe a free market. Some economists would describe the American trust of the nineteenth century as an example of free-market behavior. Let me use that example as a means to better describe the understanding of a free market presented in this book. Everyone, I hope, would agree that the use of physical violence to intimidate potential competitors or illegal bribes to bias laws is not a "free market." Many would concur that even legal use of influence by the nineteenth century trusts to obtain preferential market position (e.g., exclusive licenses or permits) was social coercion.

The definition of free market in this book extends the concept of coercive behavior to include any action directed at restraining the ability of another living power structure from prospering to the best of his ability. For example, a company should not be considered coercive for using economies of scale to reduce production cost and then setting a selling price that will maximize profit consistent with the public's demand curve. Coercion occurs when a bigger company temporarily sells a product at less than the most profitable price with the intention of permanently driving competitors from the market and then raising prices. Coercion also occurs when a company buys a patent with the sole intention of preventing others from offering products to the public that incorporate the patented innovation.

Unfortunately, the guideline of noncoercive behavior as a requirement for free-market interactions is an elusive goal. The complexity of human social and political interactions usually requires a tradeoff between different potential sources of theft. For example, a section in chapter 5 discusses the ways in which the medical license is being used to divert wealth to doctors. However, that section does not recommend allowing anyone to practice medicine. The coercion of the medical license must be balanced by the potential theft from unqualified medical practitioners. The most prosperous solution for society is the one that minimizes all sources of coercion in human affairs to achieve the freest possible market.

This complex process of minimizing self-predation in human society requires a better understanding of the role of political control in human history. Human history is a chronicle of mankind's struggle to achieve prosperity through accomplishment (motivation, education, investment, and especially innovation) and conquest (theft of the wealth of other men). These two paths to human prosperity are inseparably linked because the wealth and enhanced ability from accomplishment are incentives for conquest and because the rewards and penalties of conquest provide both strong incentives and disincentives for accomplishment. Successful conquest requires a system for exercising political control for the purpose of orchestrating political theft.

Throughout history mankind has utilized many systems for maintaining political control. The common objective of all these systems is to enhance the prosperity of the members of the controlling political power structure, usually at the expense of the other members of the larger social/political power structure being controlled. Political power structures can be categorized as either foreign or domestic, depending on the degree of common purpose they share over the group they are trying to control. Foreign power structures achieve and maintain their political control predominantly through the use or threat of physical force. However, enlightened conquerors seek to minimize the cost and maximize the benefits of political control by making their presence and control less obvious. They accomplish this objective through treaties with a puppet domestic government that collects tribute on their behalf.

Domestic political power structures, which are an important focus of this book, can be characterized in several different ways. For this book, I have chosen to characterize domestic political power structures on the basis of their control of the means of the production of wealth. We usually characterize this spectrum in terms of being "right" or "left" and I have adopted these terms as convenient abbreviations. However, for readers who find these terms offensive, you may substitute "those who control the means of the production of wealth" in place of "right-wing political power structures" and "those who do not control the means of the production of wealth" in place of "left-wing political power structures." While the constituencies that I am referring to as "right" and "left" also loosely correlate with other dimensions in the political spectrum such as "liberal" and "conservative," my use of "right" and "left" is not meant to infer these correlations.

Prior to the advent of representative democracy, the right-wing political groups that controlled the means of the production of wealth also controlled the government. However, left-wing groups were never totally unrepresented. In the Middle Ages, the church was at least a partial representative for middle-class and left-wing interests. Even earlier, the Roman republic responded to a broad spectrum of political interests. However, in all these predemocratic governments, the control of government by right-wing political groups ensured that the rules of society were biased in favor of right-wing political interests. These rules often permitted actions of legalized theft to enhance the prosperity of right-wing interests. Acts of theft by the other members of society lacked the mantle of legality and were therefore illegal, or criminal theft.

As the political process in America and in other countries has become progressively more democratic, two important political changes have occurred. First, the political line defining right-wing groups has shifted to include more of the middle class. Expansion of the right-wing political tent has occurred both as a result of concessions by right-wing political forces and as a reaction to an increase in legalized political theft by the left wing.

The second related change that has occurred in American politics has been the increasing control of government, especially the legislative branch of government, by left-wing groups. Government offers an attractive power base for left-wing groups who do not control the means of production of wealth and who therefore need another power base to exert political control over American society. The increasing left-wing control of government has been assisted by the acquiescence of right-wing political groups. The right-wing political forces in America who control the private sector and its wealth recognize the need to maintain some control over government. However, the price required to obtain sufficient popular support to elect a majority of federal and state legislators would mean relinquishing too much of the legalized theft that supports right-wing prosperity. The resulting control of government by left-wing political groups has turned government into an instrument of left-wing political theft through social programs that redistribute national income.

While the majority of middle-class Americans do receive some benefits both from the right-wing theft of corporate/governmental bureaucracy and from the left-wing theft of government programs, for the most part the middle class is the victim of theft by these two political forces. The ticket-splitting of American voters is an attempt to balance the forces of right-wing and left-wing theft by avoiding giving either group control of both the legislative and executive branches of government.

Since right-wing political power structures control the private sector institutions that create wealth in society, their systems of control and their mechanisms of theft are of the greatest historical significance. Starting with the earliest human civilizations, the rise of right-wing political power structures created conflicts within the existing social structures. These social structures were based on individuals banding together for the common good of the society. The rise of political power structures that were directed at improving the lot of some individuals at the expense of others was in conflict with the basic social contract that supported the society. Historically, right-wing political power structures have attempted to operate under the mantle of a legal framework. The legitimacy of a legal framework masks the extent of political theft, which in turn both reduces demotivation among the victims and minimizes the victim's level of dissatisfaction. Victim demotivation would reduce the pool of wealth that was the source for the political power structure's theft. Victim dissatisfaction could lead to a revolt that would require the expenditure of present wealth to suppress and inevitably reduce future wealth.

The invention of hereditary class structures was a major milestone in the development of domestic right-wing political power structures. These hereditary structures, often supported by religious beliefs as in the pharaohs of Egypt, the Brahmans of India, and later the emperors of Rome, provided a social justification for the grossly unequal distribution of wealth and authority in the society. Furthermore, hereditary class structures eliminated disorder between generations by providing a relatively smooth succession of power. However, these systems failed to provide the disorder needed for social innovation. Instead of making small adjustments as each new generation came to power, the lack of social fluidity in such systems resulted in social stagnation. This social stagnation led to periods of domestic tranquility punctuated by revolutions or foreign conquests that started a new dynasty. The history of China is an example of this process.

The four stages of feudalism are the major mechanisms of right-wing political theft throughout human history. By this expanded definition, feudalism is a mechanism of theft whereby a political power structure enhances the prosperity of its members at the expense of the other members of a society by controlling a key resource for the production of wealth.

Slavery is the first level of feudalism and its original form. Slavery is the direct control of all human labor by a feudal lord. Slavery was widely used in early human history because it was so easy to administer. However, slavery created the most resentment from the victims. Motivated men were likely to resist slavery and unmotivated men made poor slaves. Slavery was best suited to menial tasks (like rowing a galley) where obedience could be easily enforced. As technology advanced, the productive tasks in society required both increased ability and motivation. Slavery was unsuited to these tasks because enforcing quality or even production rate with a whip was very difficult.

Territorial feudalism is the second level of feudalism and the form that gave this mechanism of political theft its name. Territorial feudalism is the control of the land and all it produces by a feudal lord. The peasants had complete freedom over their lives including the freedom to starve. However, if they wanted to live, they had to work the lands of the feudal lord and submit to his control, including payment of part of their produce in taxes. Territorial feudalism replaced slavery in the Middle Ages, because feudalism provided a higher benefit/cost ratio to the feudal lord. Feudalism allowed all peasants a measure of control over their lives and rewarded peasants who had greater motivation and ability with a higher level of prosperity. The emergence of industry as the dominant force in human prosperity overshadowed but did not replace territorial feudalism. Territorial feudalism mitigated to varying degrees by societal controls is still an important factor in agricultural production, even in America (e.g., migrant farm workers).

Industrial feudalism is the third level of feudalism. Like territorial feudalism, industrial feudalism allows the workers complete freedom. However, if they wish to live, they must work at a factory under the conditions and wages specified by the industrial lord. The blatant thievery of early industrial feudalism led to violent social reactions from the workers including the union movement and the rise of communism. While the worst excesses of industrial feudalism are behind us, industrial feudalism is still very much a part of modern American society.

Professional feudalism is the fourth level of feudalism. As technology advanced, certain professional skills became virtually essential to the operation of society. Individuals who possessed those skills found that by banding together to control the supply of these vital skills, they were able to claim a much higher return than would have been possible in a free market. While territorial and industrial feudalism are still important factors in the modern American economy, professional feudalism is the most widespread form of right-wing political theft in modern American society. Virtually every profession including doctors, lawyers, educators, accountants, and trade unionists have been successful to a significant degree in controlling the free-market supply of their service and, in so doing, increasing their compensation above the free-market level. This professional thievery denies capable men and women access to these professions and denies society access to adequate and fairly priced professional services.

We face two formidable tasks as we seek to promote American prosperity through an American renaissance. Our first task is to unmask the systems of political theft in modern American society and then to evaluate those thefts to determine their impact on present and future American prosperity. Our second task is to develop both social and technical innovations that offer the promise of reducing these thefts and enhancing American prosperity. Ironically this process may adversely affect prosperity in the short run because ignorance of theft mitigates the demotivating effect of theft on the victims and because change—even gradual change—can be disruptive in the short run. However, as we have seen in the former Soviet Union, deception and social stagnation are eventually self-defeating. Lack of candor and artificial order while pacifying in the short term removes the healthy feedback needed for prosperity. The result of this policy in the Soviet Union was an endless spiral of increasing deception and eventual collapse.

Enlightened Power Structures

Enlightened power structures developed out of an understanding of the excesses of political power structures in human society. Political power structures are quasi-cancerous bodies in any social organism. Unlike biological cancers, political power structures can provide significant benefits to the society while pursuing their own interests. If the political power structures within a society provide net benefits, then the survival of the society is enhanced. If they are only mildly parasitic then, like an organism with a benign cancer, the society is less competitive, but may still survive. If the political power structures are highly parasitic then, like a malignant cancer, they likely destroy their host society and themselves as well.

Enlightened power structures are based on the understanding that freedom is the best prosperity-enhancing strategy for humanity. Freedom works because freedom motivates people to produce wealth, while denial of freedom reduces the prosperity of human societies by demotivating both the thieves and the victims. The evil of theft from an evolutionary standpoint lies not in its injustice, which is a moral perspective, but in the way theft demotivates intelligent living power structures, including mankind, from pro-ducing tomorrow's wealth. Power structures that are successful with theft (i.e., those who are able to obtain resources through theft at less cost than would be required to obtain them through work) will be demotivated from working and will instead be motivated to devote their efforts to becoming more efficient thieves. Similarly, power structures (be they individuals or groups of individuals) who have been robbed will be less motivated to produce excess wealth tomorrow. They will instead be motivated to expend time and effort to protect their wealth from thieves. Therefore, theft reduces the amount of total wealth available by diverting the productive activi-ties of both the thieves and the victims.

Human history has been driven by the interrelated develop-ment of social, political, and enlightened power structures. The previous sections have presented some examples of the interaction of social and political developments. The following paragraphs attempt to outline the development of enlightened power structures by selecting some key milestones and discussing their impact on human history. Since this is a nearly impossible task, I again ask the reader to view the entire journey rather than focus on specific milestones or conclusions.

The Exodus and the Ten Commandments mark the dawn of enlightenment in Western civilization. The release of the Hebrews from slavery in Egypt was more than an act of mercy for one people. The events leading up to the Exodus provide a clear condemnation of the practice of human slavery and support for the right of people to be free to pursue their own destiny. The Ten Commandments add a moral framework that defines the responsibilities that are an integral part of freedom. At the risk of seeming myopic, the essence of these responsibilities is imbedded in what I call the central commandment: Thou shalt not steal. The other commandments regarding murder, adultery, bearing false witness, and envy are all special cases of theft. Even the laws concerning respect for one's parents and God deal with fairness and the avoidance of theft. Similarly, the considerable text following the Ten Commandments primarily deals with rules for fair compensation. Some of these rules may not seem enlightened from our perspective, but they were major advances in enlightened behavior for those times.

The Roman Empire—in particular, the Pax Romana—was one of the most significant early successes of enlightened power structures. From our perspective, Rome was a heavy-handed political power structure, but for those times Roman rule was often very enlightened. Rome demanded obedience and tribute from captive lands, but Rome offered technology (which mitigated the effect of tribute) and a code of laws (which brought order and stability). However, the most enlightened practice of Roman society was the opportunity for people throughout the empire to earn Roman citizenship. The United States follows this practice, but many other countries still do not allow foreigners to become citizens. While books have been written on the fall of the Roman Empire, one important reason was the relentless increase in theft by the emperors of Rome and the ruling political power structures. Since the Roman Empire was a diverse culture, the altruism needed for a sense of common purpose depended on a reasonable measure of freedom and opportunity. The orgy of theft of the latter Roman Empire dissipated this reservoir of social altruism and condemned the empire to collapse.

From a purely historical standpoint, the life and teachings of Jesus had a profound impact on the advancement of enlightened power structures. The concept of human equality before God undermined both the class distinctions that were needed to support theft by domestic political power structures and the race/national distinctions that were essential to rationalize theft by imperial political power structures. His teachings of tolerance, humility, and altruism provided mankind with ideals that were in vivid contrast with the harsh realities of existing conditions. While these seeds of enlightenment initially fell on hard ground, over the years they have grown and have been a major force for the continued evolution of enlightened power structures throughout history.

The Dark Ages, which followed the fall of Rome, were marked by a preoccupation with conquest (theft of the material resources of others). Social and technological achievement ceased; and once the resources accumulated by Roman civilization were plundered, the living standards collapsed. Gradually a feudal political power structure developed based on an hereditary class structure that institutionalized the unequal distribution of wealth. While feudal society was relatively static, exceptional achievements or services to the king were rewarded by nobility often enough to motivate the population to achieve and to infuse new blood into the ruling class. The continual threat of war also restrained feudal lords against excessive theft of their subjects' wealth.

After a period of nearly a thousand years, several factors combined to create a rebirth of enlightenment in Europe. In England, the signing of the Magna Carta in 1215 began the process of broadening the political power base. In Italy the economic benefits of trade led such city states as Venice to expand freedom and to prosper accordingly. Throughout Europe, the building of cathedrals required skilled artists and tradesmen who were allowed considerable freedom to facilitate their work. In Germany, Martin Luther dramatically altered the power of the church by proclaiming that men could relate to God directly without the help of a priest.

The discovery of the New World opened economic opportunities that restructured existing political power structures and expanded the opportunities for human freedom. Men who ventured to the New World were not those of wealth and power, but those of more modest means with ambition for prosperity. The risks and distances involved necessitated that these early explorers and colonists operate with a great deal of independence. The unwillingness of existing power structures to directly conduct exploration and their inability to fully control the process led to a redistribution of wealth and a broadening of the political power base.

The enlightened thoughts of such philosophers as Voltaire struck a responsive chord among educated men in the American colonies who had acquired the vision of the frontier. A frontier is a place in space or time that is devoid of political power structures and their schemes for legalized theft. Prosperity on the frontier is based on accomplishment ("As ye sow, so shall ye reap") rather than on theft, because there are few opportunities for theft. Admittedly this scenario is idealized. We stole land first from the Indians and then from the Mexicans and cut down the forests without replanting new trees; but the major thrust of human activity was directed toward building a civilization through hard work and innovation. The background of 150 years of frontier living, the physical isolation of the American colonies, and the support of France helped the American colonists turn the world upside down and break the grip of the English power structure.

The American Revolution represented far more than the successful self-determination of a people. Many revolutions before and since have successfully overthrown foreign interests or oppressive domestic interests only to fall prey to new oppressive political power structures. The American Revolution was the first to create a society that was dedicated to individual prosperity (life, liberty, and the pursuit of happiness) and required government (and by extension, all other political power structures in the society) to serve the people's interests or be altered until it does. The success of the American Revolution was not in changing the people in charge, because all men are corruptible. The success of the American Revolution was in changing the system to provide greater freedom from human theft. The uniqueness of America has always been in knowing where we were going rather than in exalting in where we were. While a classless society dedicated to individual freedom and opportunity was more of a dream than a reality in 1776, the light of our ideals has enabled America to make continued progress in breaking down oppressive political power structures both foreign and domestic.

The French Revolution provided both similarities with and important differences from the American Revolution. The French Revolution was a reaction against the excessive theft of the ruling political power structures, the first estate (the clergy) and the second estate (the nobility). The opulence of Versailles and the extreme egotism of the nobility as depicted by their paintings and the words *"L'etat, c'est moi!"* ("I am the state") imply a loss of touch with reality. However, the French nobility were very much in touch with reality. The words of Louis XV, "After me, the deluge," clearly show that the power structures knew they were headed for disaster. The important lesson here is not only that absolute power corrupts absolutely, but that power structures are rarely able to accept innovation and save themselves from extinction. The French nobility would not compromise after the initial phase of the French Revolution, and their attempts to seek aid from the ruling nobility of Europe led to the Reign of Terror. The resulting executions virtually exterminated the nobility, thus depriving France of their considerable talents and experience.

39

The second important difference between the French and the American Revolutions was the inability of the French to establish a self-governing society. The American colonists, who were the beneficiaries of many generations of increasing self-control, were emotionally ready to accept self-government. The French, on the other hand, had always lived under authoritarian rule. While they wanted to rid themselves of political theft and could intellectually aspire to the idea of a republic, they were emotionally unable to assume the responsibilities of self-government and therefore easily fell prey to Napoléon.

Tragically, this same scenario was repeated over a century later in Russia with the rise of the Bolsheviks after the Russian Revolution. The sad truth of history is that those who are unwilling to rule themselves will inevitably be robbed by their rulers. The observation that self-government requires several generations of training needs to be remembered as we realistically assess the prognosis for the evolution of democratic governments in Eastern Europe, the former Soviet Union, and China. This lesson should not be lost on ourselves either. We are hopelessly naive if we think we can shirk the responsibility for governing ourselves and not expect to be robbed by those who assume that role.

The industrial revolution and the subsequent growth of technology created a crisis in the evolution of enlightened power structures that we are still responding to. Like exploration, the advance of technology opened up new sources of prosperity by providing methods for working smarter. However, unlike the diffuse nature of exploration, the centralized nature of technology proved very amenable to political control. Technology produced additional wealth for the resources invested, and people moved to the cities to support the factories that produced this wealth. The social issue was how the additional wealth of technology should be divided between the workers and the owners of the factories. Public attention was directed at the deplorable living conditions of the workers. However, we must remember that people chose to come to the cities because the living conditions in the cities, as bad as they were, were still better than the desperately poor conditions in the country. The important social comparison of the early industrial revolution was not the absolute poverty of the workers but the relative poverty of the workers compared to the affluence of the industrialists. This contrast was evidence of the underlying existence of industrial feudalism whereby the industrialists used their power to distort the free market for their own prosperity.

The fundamental economic issue of the industrial revolution was really the political control of capital. The excessive profits of capital resulting from control of the political power structures by the owners of capital and use of those structures to prevent a free market for capital was the basis of industrial feudal theft. The low wages of labor and the deplorable living conditions of the workers were simply some of the social results of that theft. As an example of this process consider a hypothetical clothing factory. A clothing factory requires capital investment. The cost of capital is simply a real interest (based on the perceived time value of money) plus a premium based on the risk associated with losing some or all of the principal invested. The laws of supply and demand dictate that if the rate of return from our hypothetical clothing factory exceeds the norm, then competitors will open up additional clothing factories and drive down the price of clothes until the rate of return on clothing factory capital is brought back into line. This process would increase the wage rate by increasing the demand for workers and further increase the real wage rate by reducing the cost of clothes that the workers bought.

There are several ways in which political power structures can intervene to keep the return of capital above the free-market value. One common practice is for the government to require a license and thereby directly control the number of factories. However, the most common approach is for the companies themselves to engage in predatory pricing policies that drive existing competitors from the market and thereby raise the risk premium so high that potential competitors are scared away. All this is not to deny the additional repressive effects of collusion by the ruling class to keep wages low. However, this form of legalized theft has existed throughout history and was not unique to the industrial revolution.

The American Civil War and its impact on the social structure in the South was another important milestone in the enlightenment of human power structures. The Old South was as close as America ever came to an aristocracy (hereditary-based class and power structure). We usually focus on the institution of slavery, and certainly the black slaves who occupied the lowest level in society suffered severely from this institution of legalized theft. However, the whole society was a fairly rigid pecking order where what you were allowed to do was more determined by who you were than by what you could accomplish. Like all pyramid structures, Southern society needed slavery to form the base of the pyramid. Those in the middle of the pyramid envied those at the top, but they were willing to support the system, because they benefitted from it. Slavery provided both a significant transfer of wealth from the black slaves to the rest of society and the social glue that permitted the white members to accept a severe stratification in their part of society. The abolition of slavery doomed Southern aristocracy, because the middle-class whites no longer benefitted from it.

From the Israelites in Egypt to the Untouchables in India this phenomenon of a lower caste (often of another race or religion) providing the cornerstone for a class-stratified society has been a very common occurrence throughout history. Obviously, those at the top of the pyramid benefit from a stratified society, but the strong support given these systems by the lower middle class is a phenomenon that needs further discussion. For example, less afflu-ent white males in America are among the most frequent supporters of racial and sexual discrimination (both are forms of legalized theft). If successful, such discrimination provides several apparent benefits to these supporters: (1) the discriminated are forced to take the least desirable jobs; (2) these jobs pay less than they would under a free market, thus transferring wealth to the rest of society; and (3) there is less competition for the next lowest jobs, causing them to pay more than they would under a free market. Unfortunately these benefits are largely illusory. Discrimination does create a lower class that prevents the lower middle class from being on the bottom, but the demotivating effects of such legalized theft severely restrict the economic growth of the society. In kitchen English, this preoccupation with getting a bigger piece of the pie rather than baking bigger pies results in a smaller piece of pie for everyone except the chief chef.

The rise of the union movement was in many ways a wrong turn in the search for enlightenment. The political restrictions on the free flow of capital (by both government and industry) created situations where the owners of capital could obtain profits far in excess of the cost of capital and thereby distort the distribution of wealth in society. The response of workers to this injustice by the political power structures of the capitalists was to form unions as counterbalancing political power structures of their own. While the result of the clash between these two power structures was a more equitable return for labor, these gains were offset by many losses. The chief loss was and continues to be the loss in motivation for individual excellence. Other situations directly related to this lack of profit feedback include featherbedding and restrictive job entry requirements and eventually graft and corruption. The postwar decline in union membership coincides with the growth of light industry and service industries in America. Since capital flow in these industries has been relatively free, the free market is able to provide a fair return to both labor and capital. Not surprisingly, exceptions to this trend include the education industry and the post office where capital investment is hampered by legal restrictions.

The development of monopolistic industrial power structures in America during the last half of the nineteenth century posed a great threat to the continued advance of enlightenment. The great technological advances of the nineteenth century had created tremendous opportunities for prosperity. However, control of many key technologies such as oil, steel, and the railroads had been seized by a few companies that were then able to exercise control over the market. These companies used their control to achieve profits far above the free-market return for capital. These companies maintained their monopoly positions by buying off politicians to thwart any legal reform and by briefly selling below cost (or threatening to do so) to drive competitors from the market. This legalized theft not only distorted the distribution of current wealth in America, it also stifled technical innovation in these industries. This situation if allowed to continue would have reduced economic growth and aborted America's rapid rise to prominence as a world power. This gross distortion of American's present and future wealth violated the social contract on which the American nation was based and would have ultimately led to a revolution.

The breakup of American industrial trusts by Teddy Roosevelt in the early 1900s was one of the greatest advances for enlightenment in modern times. This great achievement exhibited four very important differences from the violent transitions that marked the French and Russian Revolutions. First of all, the American political system worked. The assassination of McKinley in 1901 gave control of the ship of state to Teddy Roosevelt who was both motivated to oppose the political power of the trusts and popular enough to do so. Second, the process was accomplished by restoring a free market rather than by overcoming the power of the trusts by the power of the government. In more recent history, several American presidents have tried the latter approach with much less success; Kennedy tried jawboning the steel industry to roll back price increases, Nixon tried wage and price controls, and Carter tried excess profits taxes on oil. Third, the process avoided theft. The assets of the trusts were not confiscated. The trusts were simply forced to restructure and abide by new rules to help ensure a free market. Fourth and most importantly, the process worked in the long term. The American economy grew at a steady rate for nearly a generation until the Great Depression hit in 1929.

The Russian Revolution, which resulted in the emergence of Communism, was one of the biggest setbacks for enlightenment in modern times. Rather than promoting individual liberty, Communism sought to overcome one political power structure by creating another, only to discover that the second was as bad as the first. The whole concept of class struggle (i.e., one political power structure versus another) suffers from the same failings as the union movement, namely, the acquisition of resources by force rather than by competition in a free market. The former inevitably leads to theft since the only basis of what is fair is which side has the most political power. Similarly, the "dictatorship of the proletariat" is the same as the "divine right of kings," except for the justification used for one group to control the lives and wealth of another.

In many respects, the Russian Revolution paralleled the French Revolution. Both countries were feudal societies with a rigid social stratification based on hereditary class structures. Both societies sustained the distribution of wealth by legalized theft rather than by a free market. Both societies were driven to revolution when the economic hardship on the working class became unbearable. In France the royalty caused the revolution by their own extravagance. The Russian czar was far more paternalistic and might have stayed in power for many more years except for the severe economic deprivation caused by World War I. Both France and Russia initially formed democratic governments that fell to more radical elements, partially due to foreign intervention. Both countries fell to dictators (Lenin and then Stalin in Russia) with ambitions for foreign conquest. The Russian timetable was simply slower than Napoléon's because of the awesome challenge of rebuilding the Russian domestic economy and consolidating political power in what was already an empire of many non-Russian people ruled from Moscow. Had the rise of Nazi Germany been delayed for twenty years, the crisis of the 1940s might have been

Russian expansionism as evidenced by Stalin's 1939 pact with Hitler allowing Russia to annex both eastern Poland and the Baltic states. The defeat of Germany allowed Russia to annex large sections of Eastern Europe. The subsequent forty-four years saw many attempts to further extend this empire.

The collapse of Communism in the Soviet empire is an extremely positive event for the advancement of human enlightenment. This collapse will result in two fundamental changes: first, enhanced economic freedom and eventually political freedom for millions of people; and second, removal of any moral justification for the expansion of the Russian empire. In the near future, this process presents the monumental challenges of educating formerly captive peoples in the process of democracy and in rebuilding both the social and technical infrastructure. The reunification of Germany will provide an early indication of the magnitude of this challenge. In the long term, the collapse of Communism offers the potential for another Pax Romana where human prosperity can benefit from the combined free-market output of more of Earth's people with the parasitic cost of armaments (to protect against foreign theft) gradually reduced.

The underlying cause of the collapse of Communism was the relative failure of the Soviet system to motivate people to produce. However, the unprecedented nature of this change is that it is being performed voluntarily by the existing power structure. Such voluntary change in the face of failure is a sign of great strength, not weakness. The record of history shows that most political power structures are unable to save themselves from their own failings. Change usually comes from a domestic revolt or from external conquest. America's successful breakup of the nineteenth-century trusts discussed earlier occurred because the people regained control of the system, not because the trusts initiated the process of change. Therefore, the actions of the Soviet Communist Party to relinquish control over Eastern Europe and to democratize their society for the long-term good of their country at the expense of their own power is a very enlightened act. This enlightened act deserves our full support, because the emergence of Russia as a free and nonaggressive nation would be a significant advance in humanity's path toward enlightenment. However, the record of history suggests that such rapid transitions are often reversed. The free world must be prepared to handle such reversals and minimize their impact.

The last forty years have witnessed concerted efforts by Western societies both to contain communism and to extend domestic civil liberties. The civil rights movement and the women's liberation movement were both products of the cold war period in American society. These two processes of communist containment and expansion of domestic civil liberties were linked by both public awareness and the enlightened support of political power structures. The government focused public attention on the lack of freedom in communist societies to increase public support for the cold war. However, this process inevitably increased public awareness of civil rights injustices in our own society and sparked efforts to correct these injustices. The fear of communist expansion was also a strong incentive for domestic political power structures to exercise restraint. These power structures were enlightened enough to realize that although the cold war could be lost militarily, it could only be won economically. They realized that long-term economic growth required minimum legalized theft to motivate people to produce. Unfortunately, the removal of the external threat of communist aggression will inevitably reduce our sense of unity and common purpose. If this unleashes an orgy of theft by our political power structures, the negative impact on economic growth could easily eat up all the peace dividend from reduced expenditures on armaments.

The emerging world economy offers both promise and risk to the continued advancement of enlightenment. Foreign economic competition has had a very positive effect on many areas of our domestic economy. Foreign competition in such key industries as automobiles and steel has forced entrenched management and labor in those industries to either become competitive or go out of business. The dismantling of power structures required to accomplish this process has been painful, but many of the results are extremely gratifying (e.g., the redesign of American automobiles for higher quality and lower production cost). Unfortunately, using foreign competition rather than the American political system to overcome American political power structures is a two-edged sword. The emergence of a global economy is creating powerful global economic empires with enhanced opportunities for theft. Reaping the benefits of a global economy while avoiding abuses by the participants will be one of the great challenges of the twenty-first century.

3 / The Road to Prosperity

Life's search for prosperity and the evolution of prosperity developed the fundamental understandings needed to help us find the road to prosperity. Based on these understandings freedom from theft is mankind's road to prosperity and our road to an American renaissance. This single concept unifies the two essential aspects of human liberty, namely, the right to pursue one's life to the fullest as long as those pursuits do not infringe on the liberty of others. Freedom from theft motivates individuals to work hard for today's prosperity and to pursue education, investment, and innovation so they can work smarter for tomorrow's prosperity.

The reaffirmation of freedom as the road to prosperity is only an important first step. We need a road map in order to find our way. The next three sections present a draft for such a road map by developing more specific understandings concerning the divergent roads we have been traveling and then offering suggestions that I feel provide a more direct road to prosperity based on the principles of freedom. I view this draft road map not as final product, but as a catalyst to reawaken the innovative talents of the American people.

One of the most fundamental principles of existence is that there is always a better way. The limits we place on solutions to our social problems are of our own making, because there are no physical limits to creativity. The genesis of our misperception of limits lies in the axiom that "politics is the art of the possible." The process of social innovation is always thwarted by special interests that stand to lose favored treatment with a new system. However, neither the opposition of special interests nor the apparent absence of a better road justify discontinuing our search for one. In a free society where the rules of society respond to the democratic expression of the people, all things are possible.

A road map to prosperity is of little use if the American people do not control the direction of the car. If the chauffeurs we hire all keep taking us on divergent roads, we need to change their employment contract to make them more responsive to the American people. It also wouldn't hurt for the American people to take the wheel occasionally just to show the chauffeurs and their advisors we still know how to drive.

The Continuity of Life

The most significant contribution of the theory of evolution was the understanding that all life is part of the same biological continuum. This understanding coupled with the earlier Copernican advances in astronomy provided valuable doses of humility for the human ego and helped open the door to expanded perceptions of man's place in the universe.

This book seeks to broaden the theory of evolution with the understanding that biological, sociological, and political structures are all part of the same evolutionary continuum as cells seek to form more efficient living power structures to enhance their survival and prosperity. While each of these stages has its own unique features, they share both a common objective and a great many common features. These three levels of evolution are often highly interrelated and cannot be properly understood if they are analyzed separately, as is often the practice.

The evolution of life on Earth has been a process of increasingly complex and fractured competitive interactions. This process began a billion years ago when altruism permitted the aggregation of cells to form biological power structures that were better able to compete for survival and prosperity. This process continued with the aggregation of biological power structures to form a vast array of competing species often organized into social power structures. Mankind carried this process further with the creation of complex competing political power structures within our own species. Whenever the process of competition was positively directed, the fittest prospered most, but the overall prosperity of life improved. However, when the process of competition was negatively directed, the fittest survived, but often nobody prospered.

The fourth stage of evolution, which I have called "enlightenment," brings the process of evolution full circle. Enlightenment seeks to promote a greater sense of altruism first within the human community. This is in tune with most of the world's religions. The imagery of the fatherhood of God has the positive effect of promoting the brotherhood of man. Enlightenment offers the understanding that all mankind and in fact all life on Earth are one body whose prosperity depends on the enlightened actions of all its members.

Enlightenment espouses individual liberty as the best prosperity-enhancing strategy for humanity. Enlightenment supports return based on output ("as ye sow, so shall ye reap"), because return is the incentive for both motivation and ability improvements through education, investment, and innovation, which are the keys to prosperity. Enlightenment supports free competition, because competition is the judge and jury for new innovations. Under enlightenment, each individual is entitled only to what he or she produces. This free or theftless competition allows each person to seek individual prosperity while also promoting the overall prosperity of humanity.

The one-body concept of enlightenment requires each member to help the others achieve to the best of their abilities. If successful, this seemingly altruistic effort increases competition for available resources. However for intelligent life, the controlling limit on prosperity is the total ability and motivation of the whole body. The rising tide of prosperity resulting from increased ability lifts all boats in proportion to their contribution.

The one-body concept is tempered by the understanding that while we can help someone today, in the long term all we can ever do is help that person to help him/herself by improving his/her ability and enhancing his/her motivation. Long-term welfare is simply an unearned transfer of wealth that ultimately demotivates both the giver and the recipient.

Enlightenment rejects compulsory communalism, which is just a form of theft from those who produce more by those who produce less. Under subsistence conditions, communalism provides greater short-term survival for those whose output is insufficient to survive while not significantly demotivating those who produce more (because their net output is still at a subsistence level). However when living standards rise above a subsistence level, communalism reduces the motivation of both those of higher and lower motivation and discourages everyone from efforts to improve their ability.

Enlightenment includes the understanding that liberty is much more than the best route to prosperity; liberty is the essence of life, because an important part of the meaning of intelligent life is self-directed accomplishment. Clearly, accomplishment is essential for a meaningful existence, but this accomplishment is hollow if most of the decisions that directed it were made by others. While there must be a tradeoff between accomplishment and self-direction, the objective of parents and society in general should be to allow individuals the maximum amount of self-direction, even if others could make more prosperous decisions for them. The resulting mistakes are part of the processes of learning and growth both for individuals and for society as a whole. Political systems that deprive human beings of the opportunity to direct their own lives deprive those individuals of an essential part of life. With this understanding, even well-meaning social paternalism that deprives individuals of the ability to direct their lives comes very close to murder.

The unity of life does not repeal the need for competition and competition's most beneficial consequence, namely survival of the fittest. The process of enlightenment seeks not to prevent competition, but to include the overall impact of alternative actions in the competitive decision-making process.

The dominant role of humanity gives our species the responsibility for making decisions that affect the prosperity of all living power structures on Earth. This includes decisions that affect human social and political power structures, which will be discussed in following chapters. There will always be limited resources that require tradeoffs and decisions. Hopefully, the contribution of enlightenment is a broader perspective for making these decisions and choices. We cannot avoid this responsibility for making choices, because the decision not to choose is also a choice and usually not a very enlightened one.

Throughout the evolution of life on Earth, living power structures have sought prosperity through biological and social innovation. When these innovations gave one species a decisive advantage, that species expanded, often resulting in widespread extinction of competing species. This disruption in the natural ecosystem often impacted the dominant species as well. Eventually a new balance was restored as all species found a new stable operating point. This analogy to the dynamic response of a physical system is fundamentally accurate, because life is simply a complex interaction of living and natural chemical and physical processes. The beautiful harmony of nature is not the result of conscious design by the multitude of living power structures that comprise it, but the result of evolved patterns of biological and social interaction that were mutually beneficial (i.e., survival of the fittest on a global scale).

Even before the development of modern technology, the evolution of humanity was responsible for profound disruptions to the body of life on Earth. Mankind's first invasion of North America from Asia is linked with the widespread extinction of many species of animals, including the horse. The extinction of the horse and other native species limited the prosperity of these first Americans. Eventually a new balance was restored and native Americans evolved behavior patterns more in harmony with their environment. Ironically, the horse migrated to Asia and was a major factor in the rise of Western civilization. When Europeans began the second human invasion of North America in the sixteenth century, the horse was an important factor in their successful conquest. The escape of horses from the Spanish reintroduced wild horses to North America and permitted the Plains Indians to enjoy almost two hundred years of enhanced prosperity as horsemen until European settlers finally overran their civilization.

The recent exponential rise of human prosperity through social and technical innovations is creating a serious ecological imbalance on Earth similar to, but probably more extreme and more sudden than, any previous imbalance due to past biological innovations. The fundamental challenge that humanity faces is to use our intelligence to make enlightened decisions that will both promote human prosperity and control the impact of mankind on earth's environment. If we fail to use our intelligence and make misdirected decisions or no decisions, we will prolong and exaggerate this ecological disruption. Returning to a less advanced existence is not the road to prosperity. Banning all pesticides so less food is available and more people starve will promote neither human prosperity nor earth's ecology. Destroying all the smallpox vaccine so millions of people die of disease will not be beneficial either. Technology is the primary source of our future prosperity, but the crudeness of our emerging technology and our unenlightened use of technology are major causes of earth's present ecological imbalance.

The unrestrained expansion of humanity is the greatest current threat to the body of life on earth. All mankind's problems of pollution, urban congestion, and environmental damage are driven by the explosive increase in human population and by the desire of all the world's people for prosperity. Mankind faces an unavoidable tradeoff between the quantity of human life and the quality of both human life and all other life on earth. Technology has provided us with the means both to significantly reduce the death rate and to similarly reduce our birth rate. The issue of human population control is so controversial because our basic survival instinct resists any efforts to reduce our rate of procreation. In America the opposition of some groups to any form of population control has prevented America from playing a leadership role in the vital area of world population control. Our prosperity and the prosperity of the body of life on earth depend on enlightened decisions to regulate the growth of our species.

3.1 Recommendation: Support birth control technology and its voluntary worldwide application.
   a. Support development and worldwide application of technology that permits people to voluntarily control family size.
   b. Support revisions to both domestic and foreign policies that currently encourage large families. These policies include tax benefits, welfare benefits, foreign aid, and other incentives.

The Command and Control Structure in Human Society

The choice of a command and control structure is the most fundamental decision of all social and political systems. The command and control map presented in figure 3-1 attempts to display some of the important features of this decision on a two-dimensional plot of altruism versus authority in human social and political power structures. The command and control structure of all biological organisms is based both on absolute central authority and complete altruism between the cells. In human society, this biological model would be a beneficial dictatorship represented by the

COMMAND AND CONTROL MAP
FOR
SOCIAL & POLITICAL POWER STRUCTURES

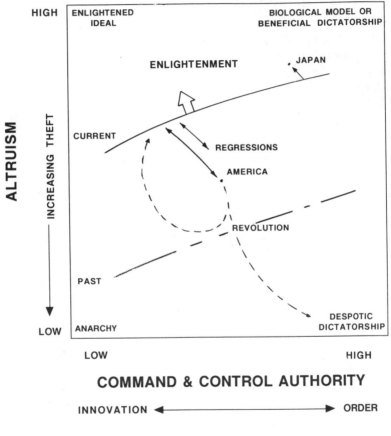

FIGURE 3-1

upper right-hand corner of the command and control map. Unfortunately no human society has ever achieved complete altruism and most early civilizations were cursed with tyrannical leaders who approached despotic dictatorships, represented by the lower right-hand corner of the map. When these civilizations collapsed, the society fell into a state of anarchy (as represented by the lower left corner of the map) with no central authority and very little feeling of altruism among the members of the society. The goal of enlightened power structures is to achieve both a high degree of altruism and a high degree of self-reliance, which minimizes the need for central control. This enlightened ideal is represented by the upper left corner of the map.

The degree of central authority correlates well with the balance between order and innovation in society. Societies with strong central control are inherently more orderly, because the central authority provides clearer direction of activity. However, societies with more individual authority are inherently more innovative because the diversity of many individuals empowered to act provides the society with many more options for social and technical innovation. For the same degree of altruism, more orderly societies have an advantage in producing today's prosperity; but more innovative societies have an advantage at improving their ability to produce tomorrow's prosperity.

By definition, the degree of altruism inversely correlates with the amount of theft in society. Societies with a strong sense of altruism have a strong sense of "one bodiness" and common purpose, which discourage theft. Conversely, societies with a low sense of altruism have a weak sense of common purpose, which encourages theft among their members. The degree of central authority determines the type of theft that occurs. With a strong central authority, the theft in society is mostly legalized theft by the members of the central authority. Conversely, societies with a weak central authority primarily experience criminal theft between the members of the society.

While stable societies have existed over a wide range of conditions, there seems to be a main sequence similar to a star map. This main sequence seems to run from middle left to upper middle right. Stable societies with more individual authority tend to be less altruistic and therefore less orderly but more innovative. Conversely, stable societies with a stronger central government tend to be more altruistic and therefore more orderly and less innovative. Over the course of human history, the main sequence line has been moving away from the despotic dictatorships of early civilizations toward more enlightened societies based on individual initiative, human liberty, and respect for the rights of others. I cannot emphasize too strongly that an enlightened society is not a communalist society. While compassion is a fundamental characteristic of enlightenment, so is free competition and a system of rewards based on "as ye sow, so shall ye reap" that promotes motivation and successful innovation.

The path toward enlightenment has been full of frequent minor regressions and occasional major regressions. These regressions begin as movements away from individual freedom toward more central control. As this process continues, altruism begins to decrease, both because the leadership is more despotic and because the people become less altruistic toward each other. This reduction in altruism leads to increases in both legalized and illegal theft in the society.

Social recovery from command and control regressions can follow two scenarios. In the first scenario, the society institutes voluntary reforms to reduce the level of theft and in so doing retraces its steps toward the stable operating point. America's recovery from the Great Depression and Teddy Roosevelt's successful trust-busing a generation earlier are examples of this path to social recovery. In the second scenario, the society falls into revolution. Revolution is preceded by a rapid drop in altruism. As an example, the American Civil War was preceded in the 1830s and the 1840s by a gradual loss of altruism between the North and the

South. However, the John Brown raid in 1859 and the election of Lincoln in 1860 caused a rapid drop in altruism that led to secession and civil war. Revolution can follow two paths. In the first path, the revolution is followed by a reduction in central authority, the institution of social changes, the slow recovery of altruism, and the eventual painful recovery to a stable operating point. However, if the pre-revolutionary drop in altruism is followed by an increase in central authority, the society can fall into the black hole of despotism. This is the path followed by Russia in the 1920s and by Germany in the 1930s.

American society is currently experiencing a major regression from stable operation. This regression is the result of several concurrent changes. First, our society has been experiencing a real loss in liberty due to encroaching central authority, together with a significant increase in both legalized and illegal theft. Second, this regression in liberty is accentuated by a movement of the American spirit toward the idea of a higher level of enlightenment. The socially unifying effects of the cold war threat have both permitted this encroachment of central authority and increased the tolerance of the American people for the resulting increase in legalized theft. However, the sudden demise of the cold war has removed the altruistic incentive of an external threat and significantly reduced the tolerance of the American people for the magnitude of our society's command and control regression from stable operation.

The social tensions posed by America's command and control regression are both a real threat and a golden opportunity for American prosperity. They are a threat because failure to decisively reverse the level of theft in our society could lead to a period of severe social unrest and economic hardship. However, American history is full of periods of crisis leading to positive changes and social renewal. Our present situation offers the opportunity for social innovations that will restore freedom to our society and propel our nation toward an American renaissance.

The discussion of command and control would not be complete without revisiting the issue of order and disorder in human society. As discussed in the first section, all power structures must provide both order for today's prosperity and disorder to permit innovation for tomorrow's prosperity. Throughout history, human societies have selected different trade-offs between order and disorder in their search for prosperity. In general, Western societies have emphasized individualism and innovation at the expense of order. These Western societies tend to be located at the left end of the command and control sequence in figure 3-1. Eastern societies, on the other hand, usually emphasize group conformity and tend to be located at the right end of the sequence. As a young boy I remember watching the movie *Alexander the Great*. In the battle scene against Darius of Persia, Alexander tells his troops that if he were to fall in battle, his lieutenants would quickly assume command (Greek individualism), but that the Persians were like a snake (strong central authority) which dies if its head is cut off. Therefore, he exhorts his troops to kill Darius and sends his outnumbered troops against the center of the Persian line. Darius flees and the battle becomes a rout. While Hollywood romanticized the movie, this historical event is an excellent example of the many clashes between more orderly Eastern societies and more innovative Western societies, which for most of human history has led to a predominance of Western societies in world affairs.

The historical reversals in the Western versus Eastern contest for supremacy are worth further assessment. The rise of China resulted in a civilization far more culturally and technically advanced than contemporary Western civilizations. The combination of a more disciplined society with a superior technology led to a rapid advance of Chinese civilization. However, the rigid central authority of Chinese society suppressed further innovations and allowed Western civilizations to catch up and surpass China. The rise of Islam several thousand years later repeated this process. The birth of Islam was accompanied by a burst of social and technical innovations, which resulted in significant advances in architecture, literature, mathematics, and metallurgy. These innovations and superior discipline fueled the expansion of Islam and almost led to the fall of Western civilization. However, again the effects of rigid central control truncated the innovative process and allowed the more disorderly but more innovative Western societies to catch up.

The United States and Japan are excellent case studies of the choices and consequences of different degrees of altruism and authority. Japan has always been a very disciplined society with strong local authority and strong loyalty to the local ruler. As Japan became united several hundred years ago, a strong common bond developed together with a strong central government under the emperor, or at least under the mantel of his authority. Just like in China many years earlier, Japan rejected foreign influences and became a relatively static society with comparatively little social or technical innovation.

The opening of Japan by Commodore Perry (United States Navy) led to a complete reversal of Japan's attitude toward technology and initiated the birth of modern Japan. While the Japanese wished to retain their social structure, they recognized the need to evaluate new technologies and to adopt those that proved beneficial. Within half a century, Japan built a modern navy that defeated the Russian Black Fleet. This gained for Japan the respect of the Western powers. Japan's adoption of modern technology was in dramatic contrast to China, which retained a middle-kingdom mentality (which we now call "not invented here") and wallowed in a medieval culture. China easily fell prey to Western colonialism and within a few years of the Japanese naval victory, the Chinese suffered a humiliating defeat in the Boxer Rebellion.

In Japan, the early part of the twentieth century saw both a return to rigid authoritarian control and the incorporation of modern technical innovations (e.g., the airplane and the aircraft carrier) into the military. The early phases of the Second World War saw the continued use of innovative technology and techniques, such as the use of carrier-launched torpedo bombers at Pearl Harbor. The mortal struggle that followed showed the response of both societies to the pressures of war. The already orderly Japanese society achieved an even greater degree of discipline. However, even more remarkably, the war changed American society from the frivolity of the Roaring Twenties and the disorder of the Great Depression to a focused and relatively disciplined society. While the Japanese retained the edge in discipline, America won the war with innovation. America entered the war with technically inferior equipment, but within a few years innovations in both equipment and tactics led to superiority in both areas. Social innovations like Rosy the Riveter (which put women on the production lines) helped fuel the production miracle in a manner that was impossible for Japanese society to emulate. In the fall of 1945 the war was headed toward the invasion of Japan and a struggle estimated to cost over a million American casualties and many times that many Japanese. The horror of the atomic explosions ended the war and provided the ultimate victory of innovation over order.

Japan's rise from the ashes of defeat to a position of world leadership has been the result of both the discipline of the Japanese people and their willingness to innovate. The introduction of democratic government provided Japan with the most powerful social innovation of Western civilization. Democratic government and a willingness of the Japanese to evaluate and adopt new ideas made Japan a fertile climate for technical innovation. First, Japanese industry adopted American quality control technology while American industry did not. Then Japanese industry adopted the transistor for consumer electronics while American industry tried to protect their investment in vacuum tubes.

Japan's ability to retain the productive efficiency of an orderly society while still vigorously pursuing technical innovations has created an engine for progress and prosperity that presents a formidable economic challenge for world leadership. As shown in figure 3-1, this achievement has enabled Japan to rise above the main sequence curve on the path to prosperity and enlightenment. While prosperity requires order, we will never outcompete the Japanese on the basis of order and discipline. America's strength and, I believe, inherent superiority is our diversity and ability to innovate. However, America's recovery and ultimate renaissance requires the removal from our society of feudal theft, which demotivates productive effort and blocks both technical and social innovations.

The Dilemma of Freedom and Theft

The dilemma of freedom is the conflict between our desire to maximize freedom to promote our own individual prosperity, while at the same time desiring to control the lives of others (i.e., restrict their freedom) so that we can profit at their expense. The dilemma of freedom is part of the broader command and control conflict that has always been a part of human society. Our bodies are composed of millions of cells all working for our common prosperity. However, American society is 240 million individuals all seeking their own prosperity. We can achieve this prosperity only two ways: by working to produce wealth or by stealing the wealth produced by others.

The Prosperity Map presented in figure 3-2 graphically displays the competing roles of work and theft in promoting prosperity and presents definitions for the terms of theft used in this book. The prosperity map is a plot of output (as measured by motivation and ability) on the vertical axis, and theft or victimization on the horizontal axis. Material wealth or prosperity, which is the sum of output and theft, is measured by the slanted dotted lines. Every society has rules that define the bounds of legality. Ideally, these should be vertical lines closely spaced about zero to minimize both legal theft and legal victimization. In reality, the lines of legality are distorted by political power structures in society to enhance their prosperity through legalized theft. The spectrum of wealth ranges from the poor in society to the middle class and finally the upper,

PROSPERITY MAP

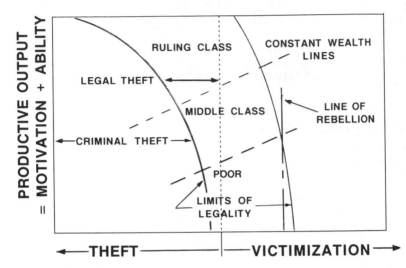

DEFINITIONS:

THEFT - INVOLUNTARY TRANSFER OF RESOURCES AT OTHER
      THAN FREE-MARKET VALUE

LEGALIZED THEFT: THEFT WITHIN THE RULES OF SOCIETY

CRIMINAL THEFT: THEFT OUTSIDE THE RULES OF SOCIETY

RIGHT-WING THEFT: THEFT BY GROUPS WHO CONTOL THE
      MEANS OF THE PRODUCTION OF WEALTH

LEFT-WING THEFT: THEFT BY GROUPS WHO DO NOT CONTROL
      THE MEANS OF THE PRODUCTION OF WEALTH

FIGURE 3-2

or ruling, class. While there are both legal thieves and victims in each class, most of the victims of legal theft are among the poor and the middle class. On the far right lies a line of rebellion that defines the limit to which people will allow themselves to be victimized. The location of this line of rebellion (which is the measure of the independence and self-reliance of the people) is the primary restraining effect on the degree of legalized theft in the society.

The prosperity map provides a means to classify various types of theft. Theft occurs whenever resources are transferred (involuntarily) at other than free-market value. The parenthetical (involuntary) is included to exclude gifts, which by definition are nontheft exchanges. Theft that occurs within the rules of society is legalized theft, which is a primary focus of this book. Theft that occurs beyond the line of legality is, of course, illegal or criminal theft. For the purpose of classification, theft has been separated vertically into right-wing and left-wing theft. Right-wing theft occurs when those who control the production of wealth in society abuse their power. They first distort the rules of society to legally permit theft and then use the rules they have created to legitimize their acts. Right-wing theft is the classic ruling power structure theft of history that primarily manifests itself in American society in the forms of industrial and professional feudalism. Left-wing theft is the abuse of popular power to distort the rules of society to permit theft. Prior to the rise of democracy, legalized left-wing theft was extremely limited. However, in many modern democracies including America, government has become an instrument of legalized left-wing theft by forcibly redistributing the wealth of society from those who earn it to those who do not. Unfortunately, both of America's major political parties are to a considerable extent hostages to political forces that advocate and benefit from right-wing and left-wing theft.

Most Americans share a strong social bond that is evidence of the altruism we feel toward our fellow citizens. We realize both intellectually and instinctively that our own prosperity is inexorably linked to the prosperity of those around us. We support laws against criminal behavior, that is all overt forms of theft, both because we wish to protect the lives of others and because we wish to protect our prosperity from such overt acts of theft. We work hard to produce the wealth needed for our own prosperity, and we are continually seeking innovative ways to work smarter so that we can achieve greater prosperity with the same or even less effort. For ourselves we seek freedom from the control and theft by others; and we also seek to promote such freedom in society, because we all benefit from the prosperity of a free society.

The production of goods and services in modern American society requires complicated interactions both among individuals and between individuals and the material resources in society. Order requires that there be rules that direct and control the inter- action of human and material resources. Inevitably almost every rule results in advantages to one group or another. This ability of the rules of society to alter the distribution of wealth creates an irresistible temptation to at least try to enhance one's prosperity at the expense of others by promoting rules that are deliberately biased in one's own interest. When these efforts are successful, the result- ing legalized theft saps the prosperity of the society nearly as effectively as the more visible criminal form. Any form of theft diverts the attention of both the thief and the victim away from productive activity toward either pursuing or resisting theft.

The insidiousness of legalized theft lies in the amoralization of such acts of theft created by the false legitimization of a legal framework. Clearly the appalling statement that "I was only fol- lowing orders," used to justify the Holocaust, represents an extreme example of such amoralization. However, the modern dictum that "you only get what you negotiate" is only slightly less absurd when used to justify the outcome of negotiations between an individual and a large organization. The presence of widespread legalized theft in any society violates the social contract that is the basis for that society. This situation erodes the sense of common purpose and eventually leads to a breakdown in the social structure.

The recent collapse of the former Soviet Union was the result of many years of oppressive legalized theft that destroyed the sense of altruism on which a sense of common purpose was based. In a recent news article about Russia, a reporter encountered a well-dressed money changer and asked his Russian friend why the man was not at work in a state job. The friend said it was common knowledge that the man had a job in a state factory at which he never worked. The man allowed his boss to pocket the paycheck he received for the phony job in return for an agreement to receive a pension in ten years when he "retired." That this scheme was viewed by many with admiration for successfully beating the system presents a sobering look at the nearly impossible task faced by Boris Yeltsin. The collapse of the Soviet Union shows that the people of the former Soviet Union no longer have a strong sense of altruism. The absence of altruism and a sense of common purpose removes the foundation for a national social unity. Like the collapse of a dying star, Soviet society is splintering in a desperate attempt to find social units small enough to achieve a sense of common purpose. The world watches and hopes this process can stabilize without the catastrophic rebound of a supernova.

Modern American society is traveling down a path similar to the former Soviet Union and, in so doing, squandering the precious investment of our sense of self-reliance and self-esteem that are cornerstones of our sense of common purpose. The relative isolation of the American frontier both forced Americans to be self-reliant and severely inhibited attempts by political power structures to institute and enforce systems of legalized theft. The freedom from theft provided by our society nurtured a strong sense of altruism and patriotic spirit. The success of early social welfare programs was due in large part to this legacy of self-reliance and sense of common purpose. People were ashamed to accept welfare and made every attempt to become self-sufficient. While there were opportunities to go to work for someone else, there were also many opportunities to be self-employed either in farming or many retail, professional, and small industrial occupations. Self-employment provided early Americans with control over their own destiny and freedom from the theft of others. Even most of the employee jobs were in small businesses where there was a close tie between the work performed and the economic value of the output produced.

The vast expansion of large corporations, powerful professional organizations, and pervasive government programs since the Second World War have gone a long way toward feudalizing American society and creating a serf mentality among large segments of the American people. The popular statement "don't bite the hand that feeds you" epitomizes this serf mentality. In a free society, the hand that feeds you is your own. While social cooperation is important, only in a feudal society do you owe your prosperity to the control and power of others. As for biting, in a free society you have the right and obligation to speak out against immorality and oppression. You also have the right to expect protection from the fear of reprisals. These concepts are fundamental to the ideals on which our nation was founded and absolutely essential to a renaissance of American prosperity and world leadership.

The only solution to the dilemma of freedom in American society is an educated and involved populace that understands the importance of freedom from theft to our overall prosperity. Freedom from theft means relinquishing our control over the lives of others and demanding that others do likewise for us. Relinquishing control means mutually forfeiting the wealth involuntarily transferred through those controls and turning our talents toward useful effort. This effort will require major reforms in the operation of government and the other political power structures in American society. However, the rewards for the restoration of freedom to American society can be a renaissance for our country based on a rejuvenation of common purpose and a revitalization of American prosperity.

The Synergism between Social Institutions and Human Behavior

Mankind is a social animal whose biological evolution has been closely linked to the evolution of human social institutions. As discussed in previous chapters, the social innovations of both written and spoken language required profound biological changes in the human brain and human vocal cords. Like ants, the prosperity of our human colony is dramatically enhanced by the cooperative efforts of millions of human beings interacting to create a human social power structure. However, unlike ants, human beings retain a strong sense of self-identity. This self-identity provides the seed for the social and technical innovations that have and will continue to dramatically enhance the prosperity of our species. However, this same self-identity contains the seed for the destruction of human society through self-predation (i.e., theft).

America's diversity is both our greatest asset and our biggest social challenge. American prosperity has been driven by the profusion of social and technical innovations that have resulted from the free interaction of the diverse cultural, ethnic, and intellectual backgrounds of our people. However, this diversity also contains the seeds of disorder because such diversity undermines altruism from biological homogeneity. No other nation has succeeded as well in creating a sense of national unity from such a diverse cross section of humanity. There are many contemporary examples of societies that have lost their altruistic glue and been devastated by civil strife. China, India, Northern Ireland, Lebanon, and recently Yugoslavia are only a few examples.

Prosperity through freedom is the basis for American unity and the great beacon of opportunity that America offers for the prosperity of humanity. From the Pilgrims to the present-day immigrants, people come to America seeking an opportunity to apply their talents and reap the rewards of their efforts in a climate of freedom. Our national motto, "E Pluribus Unum," is true on two levels. Yes, America is a great melting pot where peoples of many cultures have blended to form a more homogeneous society capable of biological altruism. However, the real source of American nationalism is not altruism born of cultural homogeneity, but altruism born of common purpose sustained through freedom. These ideals have encouraged Americans of diverse backgrounds to join the American mainstream secure in the knowledge that American freedom would permit them to also retain their cultural identity.

Blood may be thicker than water, but altruism based predominantly on biological homogeneity is neither possible for mankind nor even desirable, because diversity is needed for innovation. Japan is an example of the successful application of cultural homogeneity to achieve social altruism. This remarkable achievement has enabled the Japanese to heal the wounds of centuries of civil strife and achieve a degree of order and discipline that has made the Japanese economy a marvel of productive efficiency. While we can debate the order/disorder tradeoff in comparing the Japanese and American social models, the issue for this chapter is not which social model is better at promoting prosperity. The American model of social altruism through freedom is the only path for humanity, because the incredible diversity of our species makes a society based on the altruism of biological homogeneity impossible.

Culturally diverse societies depend on a system of freedom to nurture a sense of altruism and common interest. When social institutions support rules that promote the prosperity of the citizens obtained through their own efforts, the bond of common interest strengthens and the society prospers. However, when political power structures in the society are allowed to bias the rules to enhance their prosperity through legalized theft, the bond of common interest weakens. As this bond weakens, people are more inclined to engage in both legalized theft and criminal theft to promote their own prosperity. Social institutions reflect this change in popular attitude and either promote or offer less resistance to schemes of legalized theft by the political power structures in society. The resulting orgy of theft reduces the level of prosperity both by demotivating the citizens from producing useful output today and by demotivating increases in ability for tomorrow's prosperity.

American society is presently drowning in an orgy of legalized theft by her social and political institutions, and an epidemic in criminal behavior by individuals unable to obtain and/or maintain a legal facade for their actions. Countless societies throughout human history have fallen into similar circumstances. These societies either succumb to a violent internal restructuring or become dominated by and victimized by foreign powers. However, the framework of American society and the precedent of history show that America has the ability to restore freedom from theft to American society and continue her role as a leader of mankind. The issue we face is the same issue other generations of Americans faced: Do we have the will to restore a new birth of freedom to American society?

The success and endurance of America has been due to the flexibility of American society to respond with appropriate social innovations to counter the ever-evolving schemes of human theft. The eighteenth century was a world of territorial feudal power structures with an hereditary ruling class. America's founders clearly understood the workings of these Old World political power structures. They wisely structured our government with checks and balances to minimize the abuse of political power. Their success was greatly enhanced by the absence of territorial feudalism in the American colonies. Unfortunately, the existence of slavery in America prevented our founders from exorcising this form of feudal theft. Roughly eighty-five years after the first American Revolution, we fought a second American revolution to complete the work of our founders and rid our society of human slavery. America's founders did not anticipate either the profound role of industry on human society or the growth of industrial feudalism.

The breakup of America's trust by Teddy Roosevelt forty years after the Civil War ranks as a third American revolution.

Unfortunately, none of the first three American revolutions totally eliminated the systems of theft they were directed against. While slavery was abolished, schemes of theft directed by majority groups within American society against minority groups continue to persist. While these systems are called discrimination, implying that the minority group is being discriminated against, the real motivation is not sadism against the minority, but the enhancement of the prosperity of the majority through legalized theft. The civil rights movement of the 1960s was another skirmish in the continuing battle against the feudal institution of slavery. While the institution of territorial feudalism was officially abolished, the growth of corporate farming with labor supplied by migrant farm workers is resurrecting this scheme of feudal theft in America. Similarly antitrust laws to prevent one company from controlling a key industry have been circumvented by large and typically inefficient corporate conglomerates, which exist to promote the power of their rulers not the interest of their investors or the American public. American society is now embroiled in a fourth wave of professional feudal theft based on the control over the free market for human services. This adds to the remaining feudal baggage from the previous waves of feudal theft.

The central theme of this book is that freedom from theft is the road to both an American renaissance and a new era of prosperity for all mankind. However, freedom is not license. The proper function of a free society depends on a system of rules and incentives that create an invisible hand of positive synergism to guide individual actions toward the best interests of society. However, when the rules of society are misdirected, the negative synergism between social rules and human behavior can retard prosperity and even threaten the survival of society. The rest of this chapter discusses several ways in which misdirected rules can create negative synergism and thereby inhibit the prospects for social recovery.

Rules That Cause Conflicts between Individual Self-Interest and Social Interest

On an individual level, human behavior is most often self-directed. Human beings respond to the rules of society by developing behaviors that maximize their own prosperity consistent with those rules or at least consistent with the punishment that society imposes for breaking those rules. This self-motivated behavior bothers idealists who expect human beings to behave in the best interests of society even when such behavior is clearly not in their best interests.

Sports provide a unique window for observing human behavior, because sports strip away the social facade that often masks human interactions. Sports provide a visible contest between two individuals or groups openly acting in their own self-interest under a simple set of rules designed to direct their self-interest in the best interests of society. Several years ago when the San Francisco 49ers were headed for the Super Bowl, some of the fans complained when the 49ers would kick field goals inside the twenty yard line rather than go for the touchdown (TD). They felt that going for the TD was more entertaining (i.e., in society's best interest), and they were angry that the 49ers didn't respond to that motivation. These fans failed to grasp the reality that winning the game (i.e., prosperity for the 49ers) was the more compelling motivation. The solution to such conflicts between human self-interest and social interest in sports, as well as in society in general, is to change the rules to redirect self-interest. In fact, the rules of professional football were changed to make the goalposts narrower, which increased the incentive for trying for a touchdown.

A more pertinent example of this negative synergism is the social welfare system in America, which is full of well-meaning rules that depend on people behaving contrary to their individual self-interest. The unemployment assistance programs are flagrantly abused by otherwise honest and hardworking Americans who, not surprisingly, find themselves more motivated to find work as their benefits begin to run out. Years ago I knew several teachers who seemed to get laid off every June, collect unemployment during the summer, and then get rehired in the fall. These examples show that in comparing the working men and women of the middle class and the welfare mothers among the poor, there is no evidence of a higher morality or work ethic among the middle class. All of us are tempted to abuse the system when the rules favor our self-interest. There is menial work at low wages available to most of the people on welfare. However, the rules of the welfare system discourage working by providing a subsistence living for free and making the incremental pay for working totally unattractive.

3.2 Recommendation: Review all social rules for self-interest conflicts.

We need to thoroughly review all the rules in American society and identify those with blatant self-interest/social interest conflicts. We then need to review the social benefits these rules were intended to promote. If these benefits are still deemed vital, we need to search for alternate formulations of existing rules to minimize self-interest conflicts.

Rules That Bias Free-Market Competition Either among Political Power Structures or between Political Power Structures and Individual Citizens

The American frontier was a great facilitator for the ideals of freedom from theft that are the source of American unity. A frontier is by definition a place where human effort confronts only the challenges of nature without the organized feudal theft of others. The frontier was open land unclaimed by feudal lords and a source of opportunity for anyone willing to work it. This frontier spirit extended to industry and all forms of human endeavor. Unfortunately, the American frontier was finite; and as fences grew across the American landscape to protect territorial interests, similar fences grew across our industrial and professional landscapes. While everyone recognizes the utility of fences, their existence needs to be tempered by common social interests such as free passage, water rights, etc., lest the private right to fences leads to territorial feudal control. We have developed a body of law to temper public and private territorial rights, but we have been much less successful in controlling the profusion of fences across our industrial and professional landscapes.

3.3 Recommendation: Review all social rules for special interest bias.
We need to thoroughly review all the rules in American society and identify those with blatant special interest bias. These especially include rules that support industrial restrictions on the free market and rules that impose professional restrictions on the free market. We then need to rereview the social benefits these rules were intended to promote. If these benefits are still deemed vital, we need to search for alternate formulations of existing rules to minimize special interest bias.

Rules That Direct Political Power Structure Behavior toward Self-Perpetuation Rather than toward Useful Output

The profit motive of the private sector provides a natural mechanism to redirect resources toward activities that are the most in demand. However, the public sector, which has no such mechanism, tends to accumulate the useless baggage of organizations that have served their purpose and now are directed at self-perpetuation.

3.4 Recommendation: Review all public agencies for usefulness.
We need to review the objectives and operation of all public agencies to identify both duplication of effort and unnecessary effort. We

75

then need to vigorously prune the dead wood of useless agencies and merge agencies that needlessly duplicate function.

Rules That Perpetuate Gross Size Imbalances between Competitors in the American Free Market

Free-market competition can only exist when the competitors are of roughly equal size. While there are economies of scale, there are also diseconomies of scale due to bureaucracy and loss of innovation. Most political power structures grow well beyond the free-market optimum size to obtain control over the market.

3.5 Recommendation: Review political power structure size imbalances.
We need to examine the size of all political power structures in American society and determine whether size imbalances exist that significantly affect free-market competition. Where such size imbalances are found, society needs to divide these power structures to restore free-market competition and enhance the climate for innovation.

The synergism between social rules and human behavior is such a strong force in human development, because humanity is both thoroughly social as a species and incredibly independent as individuals. On a positive note, human independence is the motivation for both innovation and the vast array of political power structures that efficiently perform specialized functions in human society. Unfortunately, human independence undermines the altruistic glue that directs individual behavior toward the broader social interest. Therefore, the prosperity of human society depends on the successful implementation of the rule of law. When properly formulated, the rule of law discourages individuals from behaving contrary to the broader human social interest. However, when improperly applied, the rule of law can actually facilitate antisocial

76

acts of individual self-interest either by failing to address certain acts of theft or by providing the mantle of law to actually support those acts.

The corruption of the rule of law and the legalized theft this corruption supports are fundamental road blocks to our American renaissance. Corruption of the rule of law has been an integral part of human self-predation throughout history. This phenomenon was well understood by the founders of America and their under-standing helped guide the early history of our republic. Therefore, we need to better understand the factors contributing to the perva-sive corruption of the rule of law in modern American society. I believe the corruption of the rule of law in America has at least three sources: (1) an overly idealistic view of the nature of man, (2) the complexity of modern society, and (3) a decline in American self-reliance, leading to an excessive dependence on central author-ity.

The relative isolation of America and our success at forging a reasonably tranquil society from many diverse interests have given us an overly optimistic and somewhat naive perspective on human nature. We can read about the strife in Northern Ireland, the geno-cide in Cambodia, and the atrocities in Yugoslavia, but we cannot really appreciate their significance. Even the periodic riots in America's inner cities seem somewhat unreal to us. Our emotional isolation is a strength, because it permits America to pursue human ideals that would not even be considered in other countries. On the other hand, our detached perspective is also a dangerous weakness if it causes us to misjudge the self-directed nature of our species. Allowing doctors to regulate society's interests in medicine, law-yers to regulate society's interests in law, and commercial interests to regulate society's interests in business is hopelessly naive for the present state of human development, even in America.

Secondly, the increasing complexity of modern life has been a strong factor in the decline of popular participation in the direction of the rules of American society. The explosion of knowledge in both the sciences and the social sciences and their complicated interactions in modern society leave the average citizen with a feeling of inadequacy. The political apathy we see in America is due at least in part to the intimidating complexity of modern life. Unfortunately, the catatonic withdrawal of American citizens from the political process has left a power vacuum that is being filled by those who would distort the rules of society for their own profit at our expense. The solution to this dilemma is known to every chief executive officer (CEO) in America. The CEO delegates the daily decisions to the experts (i.e., our elected representatives), but the CEO stays in the picture to make the major long-term policy decisions. Extension of the popular initiative process to the national level with decisions requiring a supermajority vote is the best way to restore citizen oversight to the long-term direction of American society.

Third, the most ominous factor contributing to the present corruption of the American political process is the decline in the level of self-reliance of the American people. Self-reliance and the spirit of individualism are essential both to the process of political democracy and to the processes of social and technical innovation that a free society promotes. Unfortunately, both our evolution as biological power structures and our continued evolution as social power structures drive us toward a centralized command and control structure. The compelling preference of living power structures for strong central authority can be observed from the top dog behavior of wolves and domesticated dogs to the kings and emperors of early human history.

The survival of self-reliance in America can only be achieved by social structures that allow individual Americans to control and direct their own lives. The most important factor in the success of the American Revolution was the superior degree of independence and self-reliance of the American people. This self-reliant attitude was not a fluke of nature but a direct result of the social environment of frontier life in the American colonies. The American frontier and its magnetic effect on risk-taking immigrants from around the world continually nurtured a self-reliant attitude in the American character. The closing of the American frontier in the nineteenth century and the maybe-not-so-coincidental growth of centralized authority (big companies, big government, big unions, big corporate farms, big cities, and pervasive national organizations) in the twentieth century have, I fear, done major damage to the sense of self-reliance in the American spirit. We cannot endure as a nation of independent and self-reliant individuals if we continue to live in a social structure that requires us to forfeit control of our daily lives to central authority. Since the option of a beneficial dictatorship is neither possible in human society (due to the diversity and lack of altruism of humanity) nor desirable (due to the loss of innovation that would truncate the ascent of man), we must act to reduce the level of central authority to preserve the American dream for ourselves, our children, and for all humanity.

4 / The Four Tires of Prosperity

Motivation

Motivation is the most fundamental of the four tires of prosperity. Motivation is the incentive for all prosperous activity. Motivation determines how hard we work with our current abilities to produce today's prosperity. Motivation also provides the incentive to improve our abilities through education, investment, and innovation to enhance tomorrow's prosperity. Therefore, the most fundamental issue for both individual prosperity and the overall prosperity of the human social power structure is how to provide incentives to motivate human behavior toward prosperous activity.

Motivation has three distinct yet overlapping sources. These three sources of motivation are fear, pleasure, and accomplishment. These three sources form ascending steps in the quest for enlightenment. Fear is the bottom motivational step and the basis for the vast majority of biological motivation. Pleasure forms the middle step and provides a transitional source of productive incentive. Accomplishment, specifically self-directed accomplishment, provides the most enlightened source of motivation.

Fear is really an emotional response based on the anticipation of pain. Pain and its precursor (fear) are nature's way to discourage nonbeneficial activities and direct effort toward behaviors that enhance survival and prosperity. Hunger, thirst, excessive heat or cold, bitter- or sour-tasting foods, foul smells, heights, deep water, and of course the sight of predators are all stimuli that motivate biological power structures toward pain-aversion activities.

Fear is most effective as a motivator under subsistence conditions, because future orientation is not a widely distributed characteristic. Like the grasshopper and the ants, most biological power structures (including man) rapidly lose fear motivation as soon as present conditions become reasonably comfortable. The scarcity of future orientation is evidence that natural selection has not favored excessively future-oriented behavior. Prior to the advent of civilization and technology, rainy day savings was the only motivation for producing in excess of daily needs. Therefore, natural selection favored behavior to provide for normal emergencies (like winter), but natural selection did not extend the fear motivation beyond conditions of normal need.

The sensations of pleasure provide the second step of motivational incentives. The pleasure of good food and good company, not to mention warm and secure shelter and, of course, the many pleasures associated with reproduction and parenting, are all strong positive motivators to perform these prosperity-enhancing behaviors. The sensations of pleasure overlap the sensation of fear to produce both a continuum and a prioritization of motivational incentive. We respond first to fear and then, in the absence of fear, we respond to pleasure.

Humanity has adopted pleasure as the solution to the motivational crisis caused by the advance of civilization and the gradual removal of fear-motivated behavior. The creation of holidays and religious festivals for rest, renewal, and enlightenment was an important early use of pleasure as a motivator in place of fear. Modern civilization has built on this concept with weekends and the paid two-week vacation. The pleasure of good food has led to a proliferation of good restaurants, the pleasure of good company has led to a wide variety of social outlets, and the pleasure of secure surroundings has led to a vast expenditure of effort on homes, schools, and a supporting social infrastructure.

While pleasure is not an unworthy source of motivation, the nearly exclusive reliance on pleasure for motivation is a perversion of modern human civilization. While fear is a totally sufficient motivator for prosperous activity, pleasure is not. Since fear is an aversion response, mankind is in no danger of abusing this source of stimulation. However, the positive sensations of pleasure present an almost irresistible temptation for abuse. The negative consequences of the abuse of pleasure have been and continue to be one of the greatest threats to both individual human prosperity and the overall prosperity of human society. The negative consequences of pleasure abuse range from the relatively benign consequences of obesity to the hellish consequences of hard drug abuse. The pleasures derived from material wealth more so than fear of their absence are the primary motivators of the many schemes of legal theft in modern American society and throughout human history. Similarly, the pursuit of pleasure by the ruling classes in human societies has been the primary motivation for the self-predatory wars that have so ravaged our species.

The rise of technology offered mankind a whole new dimension of ability improvement and prosperity enhancements obtained through working smarter. Industrial production is one of the most important means by which technology promotes prosperity. Industrial production increases the rate at which material goods can be produced and thereby reduces the labor input required for each item. In a free market for labor and capital, industrialization leads to the flow of capital to the most productive and profitable uses. This also leads to an increase in the wages paid for labor in those industries.

The increased production efficiency achieved by industrialization required an increase in the demand for industrial products. Initially the demand for many basic industrial products (e.g., clothing and building materials for basic shelter) was motivated by fear. The ability of technology to make these items more easily available enabled increasingly large segments of humanity to achieve a higher standard of living and thereby escape fear motivation.

The desire to raise all members of society above a fear-motivated existence has led to an even further emphasis on pleasure as the source of human motivation. As the standards of living continue to improve through advances in technology, large segments of humanity are able to move economically from fear motivation to pleasure motivation. However, continued advancements in material prosperity require both increases in productivity to increase the wage rate and an increase in total production both to pay for the investment in tools and to actually pay workers a higher income. Increased production requires increased consumption of industrial products to support increased industrial production. Since mercifully technology had raised the standard of living for most of American society well above the level of fear motivation, pleasure motivation was the only available incentive for increased consumption.

Marketing employs several strategies to increase pleasure-motivated consumption of industrial products. We are urged to buy more of the same thing (e.g., two cars, two TV sets, etc.). We are urged by buy new things (e.g., microwave ovens). We are urged to consider old items as obsolete (e.g., old cars) or out of fashion (e.g., old clothes). Finally, we are urged to buy more complicated versions of familiar items (e.g., cars with air-conditioning, hi-fi systems, and cellular phones). The social basis for all these marketing strategies is mankind's struggle to raise all members of society above a fear-motivated existence through high value-added labor using industrial production. Unfortunately, this effort to liberate all humanity from fear motivation through material consumption drives the more affluent members of society uncomfortably deep into a pleasure-motivated life-style.

The quality-of-life movement represents humanity's search both for a more complete definition of prosperity and for a deeper meaning to life than the mindless pursuit of pleasure. About thirty years ago, the American public began to seriously oppose the consumeristic emphasis on the quantity of life in favor of more emphasis on the quality of life. This movement was led by young people who had grown up in the affluence of the post-war 1950s and who had a different perspective on fear motivation than their parents.

In the 1930s one of the campaign posters for Franklin D. Roosevelt showed a factory with tall smokestacks belching black smoke. Even at that time people knew that air pollution was harmful. However, the smoke meant employment and a release from the poverty-driven fears of the depression. The quality-of-life movement is part of the enlightened awareness that prosperity is more than gross national product and the meaning of life is more than pleasure. However, this movement needs to be tempered by the realization that with our emerging technology most of humanity still has the wolf of fear nipping at their heels. Part of this tempering process deals with a broader understanding of material wealth.

Wealth is the sum total of the state of ordered matter on Earth. The physical elements that comprise the Earth include some of the lighter, higher potential energy elements from the creation of the universe; but more predominantly, the Earth consists of the heavier, lower potential energy elements from the ashes of stellar furnaces and their cataclysmic demise. Since all closed systems move from a more orderly state to a more disorderly state, the creation and even the preservation of wealth requires energy. The energy released by the gravitational consolidation of the Earth and the light from our sun have provided the predominant sources of energy for our Earth. This energy occasionally resulted in the creation of more ordered structures of matter, in particular organic matter; but for the most part, the early Earth was a barren planet.

The origin of life began the systematic creation of wealth on Earth. The very essence of life is the ability to use energy to enhance the ordered state of matter. The gradual evolution of life, first in the seas and then on land, has created a profusion of ordered matter in the thin layer we call the biosphere. With the important exception of the shells of marine organisms, most of the wealth produced by living power structures was in the form of living tissue. When these living power structures died, their tissues were dismantled by living processes and ultimately reconstituted in even more highly ordered states. Thus the evolution of life on Earth has continually reused the finite reservoir of terrestrial carbon to create ever more complex and valuable arrangements of living tissue.

The emergence of intelligence led to the use of the creative powers of life to rearrange nonliving matter into progressively more ordered states. From the pyramids of Egypt to the sprawling cities of the twentieth century, the rise of human civilization is carrying the creation of ordered states of nonliving matter to new levels of sophistication. However, when the construction of a city means the destruction of a forest, the creation of wealth through the addition of ordered nonliving matter is partially offset by the loss of wealth through the destruction of ordered living tissue. This process requires an appreciation of both forms of wealth and an enlightened tradeoff. I believe our ancestors understood this tradeoff when they used the word "conservation" to denote both the preservation of natural wealth and the development of humanity's artificial wealth.

The quality-of-life movement combines the conservational appreciation for natural wealth with an overwhelming sense of guilt over modern society's excessive emphasis on pleasure motivation. This sense of guilt biases our judgement concerning tradeoffs between natural and artificial wealth, and leads to illogical statements like, "Mankind is a blight on the planet." We should all view with concern the loss of natural wealth caused by human development to support our exploding numbers. However, our perspective needs to consider the vast majority of humanity who is still struggling to escape fear motivation. Since we have not experienced the fear motivation of our parents nor do we experience the fear motivation of most of humanity, we have a distorted view of the contribution of artificial wealth to human prosperity. The consumption of Earth's natural wealth by mankind is the result of (a) too many people, (b) humanity's motivation for a higher standard of living, and (c) our emerging technology that inefficiently uses natural resources to meet human needs. The solution to human prosperity is both better technology and better directed technology using a free market that should include democratically established social costs as free-market incentives.

The selection of government power in the 1960s to promote the quality of life helped fuel the present explosion of both right-wing and left-wing theft in American society. The use of government power to handle crisis situations like wars and the Great Depression is a necessary expedient, because free-market controls usually take longer to develop. However, the continued use of government power to control social decisions is destructive to individual freedom, which is the basis of American prosperity. Government power places economic tradeoffs in the hands of central authorities whose prosperity is determined by the further enhancement of government power, not by the free-market control of the American people. Furthermore, government power by definition substitutes fear motivation (fear of the law) for any free decision-making process.

As an example, the free-market approach to pollution control should have been and can still be used to establish by democratic means a social cost associated with air pollution. This social cost should rationally vary by both the type of pollutant and its location. For example, the social cost of air pollution would be higher in Los Angeles than in the middle of Nevada. Industries and individuals could select the level of pollution control based on the penalties they would otherwise have to pay. The social costs set by society would provide the research and development incentive to devise better and less costly means to control pollution. Drivers of private automobiles could elect to reduce their air pollution penalties by (a) driving less, (b) buying a car that gets better mileage, (c) buying a car with better pollution controls, or (d) moving to an area with lower pollution penalties. This same free-market approach would also work for gasoline consumption. Assuming that there is a social cost associated with gasoline consumption other than pollution, a tax on gasoline provides a free-market disincentive for its consumption. While technology and a free-market, together with reasonable controls on human population, offer a path to lift mankind above a fear-motivated existence, technology does not offer the answer to the guilt and loss of purpose resulting from modern America's excessive reliance on pleasure motivation.

The solution to modern America's excessive reliance on pleasure motivation is to rediscover the tremendous motivating powers of accomplishment. For this discussion, accomplishment is defined as "the creation of wealth or the enhanced understanding of how to create wealth." While all wealth is tangible because wealth involves more ordered states of matter, knowledge is a high form of accomplishment. New knowledge is the enhanced understanding of the laws of the universe that determine the ways in which matter can be ordered. This enhanced understanding provides direction in the creation of more ordered states of matter with less expenditure of energy.

The sense of accomplishment is the third and most enlightened source of human motivation. The sense of accomplishment is a direct result of the creation of more ordered states of matter or of the knowledge of how to do so. Social interactions are also an important source of human accomplishment, because education whether from parents, teachers, or friends enhances the order of the mind and body. The sense of accomplishment obtained from these activities requires neither the whip of fear motivation nor the treat of pleasure motivation.

There is no better example of the motivational vacuum that exists within many of America's large corporations than the sign, so often tacked to company bulletin boards, that reads, "The worst day of fishing is better than the best day of working." For the many individuals who agree with these sentiments, work offers little or no sense of accomplishment. For them, work is simply a task to be endured to obtain money to support the pleasure of leisure activities like fishing and Monday night football. There is nothing wrong with enjoying the pleasures of life, because pleasure is one of nature's important motivational rewards. However, a society in which many individuals' prosperity-enhancing activities bring little or no sense of satisfaction and accomplishment is a society that has taken a wrong turn on the road to prosperity.

The prosperity of the United States is to a very significant degree due to the motivation provided by the sense of self-directed accomplishment. The American frontier provided both an environment that was free from the theft of feudal power structures and the opportunity to experience the thrill of self-accomplishment. America is no longer a frontier society, and our more crowded conditions require social cooperation and teamwork. However, true teamwork is really the coordinated efforts of individual excellence. True teamwork that provides for self-directed accomplishment obtained through theftless competition is the most satisfying form of motivation. However, the call for teamwork in hierarchical structures is hypocritical if the hierarchy uses its power to distort the reward structure.

There is an inherent conflict between the concentration of power and wealth in feudal hierarchical power structures and the opportunity for either freedom from theft or a sense of accomplishment by the workers in these systems. Large social structures work better in countries like Japan where there is greater altruism. However, in Western society we have less social altruism and more individualism that provides the seed for innovation. However, these conditions turn our large social structures into political power structures motivated by the prosperity of those in control.

Enhancement of sense-of-accomplishment motivation in America requires downsizing America's large political power structures to permit more people to experience a sense of self-accomplishment. This movement away from large political power structures to small political power structures also mitigates the opportunities for feudal theft in society. Downsizing of political power structures requires a smaller, more privatized government at all levels, as well as fewer large corporations and many more small businesses and self-employed individuals. This double motivational benefit of an enhanced sense of self-accomplishment and a reduction in legalized theft will strengthen the motivational tire carrying us to an American renaissance.

Education

Education may very well be the most profound sociobiological innovation in the entire evolution of life. Before education, all biological behaviors were directed by instructions encoded in the DNA. The only way to improve these behaviors was by random changes that were then either favored or eliminated by natural selection. The invention of education allowed living power structures to improve their behaviors through knowledge acquired during their lifetimes. Initially this knowledge was from direct experiences with the world. However, as life evolved, education expanded to include indirect experiences and favorable behaviors transmitted from one generation to another via parents or teachers. The invention of written language by our species further expanded the power of education. Written language permitted a more detailed record of experiences and enabled experiences to be transmitted using written materials from teachers who were absent or even no longer living.

The profound nature of education requires that this chapter start with a big-picture assessment. Life is a continual process of education. Every waking moment, every experience or social contact provides input that we use to improve our ability to more effectively deal with the world. We have twenty-four hours each day to experience the world, and the challenge we face is how to use those hours most effectively. Human activities are normally broken down into three categories: work (use of abilities to produce today's prosperity), education (investment in improving our ability for tomorrow's prosperity), and pleasure (use of time and material resources for the enjoyment of life not specifically related to work or education).

The following discussion of pleasure and the activities we pursue for pleasure builds on the discussion in the previous chapter and provides some valuable insights into deficiencies in the activities we pursue for work and education. The fundamental question of pleasure is the source of our motivation for activities that often appear to be unrelated to either present or future prosperity. Pleasure involves behaviors that produce physical responses that we are biologically conditioned to find rewarding. We need to try to understand the biological basis for this conditioning before we try to make value judgements on the apparent frivolity of pleasure-time activities.

Sleep is by far the most time-consuming pleasure activity. Sleep originated as a diurnal hibernation activity to conserve energy during the nighttime hours when darkness both prevented normal activities and increased the danger from predators adapted for nighttime hunting. Sleep provided a convenient time for biological refurbishments that then permitted more sustained activities during daylight hours. In higher animals, sleep provided a time to mentally sort out the day's activities through the process of dreaming. With modern civilization, we have lights that permit nighttime activity and we are no longer threatened by nocturnal predators. However, these modern conveniences do not eliminate the basic biological functions of sleep, namely physical and mental renewal. Only by thoroughly understanding these biological functions can we hope to develop methods to reduce the required amount of sleep and thereby expand the number of waking hours in the day available for prosperous activities.

All the other so-called pleasure activities also have a basis of biological utility. The pleasurable process of eating is necessary for refueling. Exercise and sports provide physical conditioning that is often missing in our sedentary work activities. Socializing maintains the fabric of our social power structures and provides us with information and language skill practice (both educational functions). Travel provides a stimulating educational experience. Recreation provides physical stimulation missing in normal activities and a sense of renewal missing in the alien artificial environments we often work and live in. Finally, hobbies provide us with a sense of accomplishment often missing in the narrowly focused work activities of modern civilization.

The issue with pleasure, as with all other activities including education, is defining the proper balance of time and resources for each activity. Oversleeping robs our lives of time for prosperous activities. Overeating reduces our physical abilities and impairs our health. Similarly, abuse of pleasure-producing or stimulating substances (e.g., sweets, alcohol, coffee, and tobacco) or illegal drugs reduces our ability to prosper. An important educational objective for a free society is to help people learn to evaluate the relative benefits of life's many activities and to make intelligent (i.e., prosperity-enhancing) choices on the allocation of their time and resources among those activities.

The big picture view of education shows that formal education is only part of the lifelong process of learning personal ability improvement. Modern society is an experience of information overload. We have books, magazines, newspapers, music concerts, art exhibits, museums, theater, movies, radio, and of course television. In a free society, our choice of educational alternatives determines the knowledge base that will strongly influence our own prosperity; and our vote also helps determine the mix of educational experiences that are available to others. Therefore, another objective of the educational process should be to help people learn to evaluate the information they are receiving and to avoid overdosing on sugar-rich material whose empty calories provide short-term excitement, but do not provide the basis for prosperity-enriching experiences.

The origin of formal education was for specialized training in written language and theology to prepare men for the clergy or for positions of secular authority. The general population was illiterate. Those who worked at skilled occupations learned their skills through apprenticeship programs. Early public education was directed at fundamental skills (e.g., reading, writing, and arithmetic) that promised a high return both to the student and to society. The tremendous value of education to economic prosperity has led in the last century to a virtual explosion in the resources devoted to formal education. Unfortunately, this explosion has created a system that is in many respects out of touch with the educational needs of American society.

The purpose of formal education is to develop the abilities of the young through the acquisition of knowledge and specialized skills to promote their prosperity and thereby promote the prosperity of society. While prosperity may be broadly defined, education should be objectively directed. I believe that formal education has three fundamental educational objectives and two important supporting social objectives. The three educational objectives are career development, societal interaction skills, and cultural appreciation. The two supporting social objectives are to provide a screening process for social placement and a holding tank for social maturation.

Career Development

The primary purpose of formal education must be the development of career skills that a free market will find useful. The purpose of education is not simply to prepare a student for more education. The almost total absence of any discussion of career planning in modern education is an absolute travesty of the objectives of education. In the seventh grade, I decided that I wanted to be an engineer. This decision both motivated me to work hard in junior and senior high school and focused my attention toward the academic skills I would need for the engineering profession. My parents also strongly encouraged me to do well in English, because ideas are of no value if one cannot articulate them. The motivation and direction of my career focus formed the basis for my successful college work and professional career in engineering.

The process of formal education should include a continual assessment of career planning. The school system needs to help the student ask and answer the following questions: What are you talented in? What do you enjoy doing? What types of careers require these talents? What special skills do they require? What do they pay? The school system then needs to go beyond these easy questions to the real question: Do you realistically have the motivation and talent to acquire sufficient proficiency in these skills to be successful in that candidate career?

School systems avoid the process of career assessment, because every parent wants their child to go to college. Rather than help the student and the parents realistically measure and direct their child's career potential, the schools duck the issue of career planning. When I graduated from high school, the state university was required by law to accept every student with a high school diploma. However, marginal students were required to take a brutal summer English course that many of them failed. The university used this method both to reduce the size of the freshman class and to screen out students who were really not college material. Failure of summer English abruptly threw these students into the job market with no specific job skills and with an initial feeling of failure. The present educational system extends this process by encouraging many of these students to spend several years in junior college before finally seeking a career they should have been prepared for in high school.

4.1 *Recommendation: Require career planning in secondary school.*
Schools should be required to provide students with comprehensive

career planning starting in junior high school. This planning would include an honest annual assessment of the students' abilities and career prospects.

The lack of career planning and vocational training in high school is at least in part due to resistance of trade unions that seek to control the supply of individuals able to compete for vocational jobs. The issue of union representation of workers must be separated from the ability to decide who can join the union. The school systems should both provide vocational training in a wide variety of skills and coordinate this training with apprenticeship programs so that high school students not going to college would have a marketable skill when they graduate. Federal and state laws should require unions that represent these trades to accept graduates from these programs into their membership.

4.2 Recommendation: Require vocational training and certification.
Schools would be required to offer programs of vocational training (either at school or contracted out) as part of a vocational degree program. These programs would lead to state certification of at least entry level competency in each field. State law would mandate this certification as sufficient for entry into any union representing workers in that field.

Social Interaction Skills

Social interaction skills are the next most important objective of formal education. These skills include reading, writing, public speaking, basic mathematics, and basic science. Students headed for college will, of course, concentrate in these areas; but even these students miss training in fundamental skills deemed to be too practical. In English, along with the study of great literature, schools should include more emphasis on expository writing and business letters, as well as writing and presenting speeches. Course work should include essential social skills such as handling a checkbook, understanding and handling credit, understanding insurance, filing a tax return, interviewing for a job, and understanding basic legal requirements and rights. Science courses should ensure technological literacy as well as theoretical competency, even for college-bound students. For example, students should understand the basic operation of an automobile and major home appliances. Just because these skills are not required to get into college does not mean they are academically unworthy.

4.3 *Recommendation: Require social interaction skill training.*
Schools would compile a list of social interaction skills needed for an adult to function in modern society and would offer training in these skills. Students could opt out of this training by passing tests on each skill, but would be required to master all skills to graduate.

Cultural Appreciation

Formal education has a responsibility to provide students with an understanding and an appreciation of human culture. This includes the study of history, government, foreign languages, art, and music. In general, school systems spend sufficient time presenting this material. However, various studies indicate that student retention of this material is often lacking. I am personally grateful for the educational experiences I received in cultural appreciation. I found this knowledge extremely valuable, both for social interactions as well as for my career in engineering. Furthermore, I would not have been able to write this book without a basic education in human culture.

Screening Process for Social Placement

One of the most important, though largely unacknowledged, functions of formal education is to provide a screening process for social placement. Social power structures are like a tree. Each branch represents a different talent, such as musical ability, athletic ability, spacial reasoning ability, etc. Talented individuals may simultaneously exist on several branches. A fundamental challenge of society is to properly place individuals on the branches, much as players on a tennis ladder. The formal education process is like a marathon where the students compete against each other. Over time students spread out as they either distinguish themselves or fail to do so in various fields. Those who excel in high school may choose to go on to college where the screening process repeats itself. When these students flow into society, their educational attainment provides the basis for initial social placement. Their degrees and the transcripts that support them are indicative of the mastery of specific skills. However, just as important, academic ranking is indicative of an individual's relative ability to handle work and responsibility in society.

Unfortunately, there are groups in American society that seek to remove all indicators of individual distinguishment based on superior effort and accomplishment. In school systems, this leads to pressure for pass/fail grading systems with very few failures and automatic promotions. Under these systems, a high school degree is nothing but an attendance certificate and worthless for guiding social placement. Therefore students go to junior colleges, four-year colleges, and even graduate schools in an attempt to distinguish themselves from their peers. The basic issue of "What ability improvements am I going to obtain by going to college?" gets lost in the objective of obtaining a college or even graduate degree.

The motivation to attend college in America is largely driven not by the desire to obtain training in a specific field or even the desire to gain knowledge or broader cultural understandings. The motivation to attend college for most students is simply to obtain the social placement credential represented by a college degree. However, as more and more students obtain college degrees, the social placement function of the college degree becomes devalued.

Ironically, the debasement of academic credentials has been paralleled by an increasing reliance by society on the college degree for employment. Employers desperately need some measure of an applicant's motivation and ability to use as a basis for hiring. As academic credentials become debased, employers require junior college degrees for positions that used to only require a high school diploma, and college or even graduate degrees for positions that really do not require that level of academic achievement. This situation is leading to a vast misallocation of national resources to higher education. This misallocation occurs both for students who do not need a college education for their careers and for courses that may be enlightening, but which have little relevance to the student's future prosperity or to the prosperity of American society.

4.4 Recommendation: Restore the value of a high school credential.
All prospective high school graduates would be required to take a national test to demonstrate competency in basic verbal and mathematical skills. Like the SAT, these tests would be numerically graded. Individual states would be permitted to set their own minimum requirements. Students' transcripts would show their test scores (as well as their grades), and the statistical compilation of the test scores would be available by school, school district, and state for public review. Students could retake the examination even after graduation with the results and dates of all tests appearing on their transcript.

4.5 Recommendation: Ban discrimination in hiring based on a college degree.
Employers would be required to define specific job skills as being necessary for a specific position. They could use successful completion of college-level courses in each discipline as evidence for

fulfilling each job skill requirement. However, they could not simply use a college degree as a job requirement. This recommendation would force students and universities to consider career job skill requirements in formulating their degree programs. This recommendation would also permit nondegreed candidates to prepare for careers by acquiring the specific skills required for that occupation.

The debasement of educational credentials is echoed by the legal restrictions being placed on employment records as a guide to future employment decisions. Anonymity strikes at the very heart of individualism by discouraging motivation and ability improvements needed for prosperity. Most of our public sector employees are paid based on time in grade with little opportunity for reward based on excellence. Loss of individualism is also one of the most detrimental effects of unionism. Depriving individuals of the right to establish a record of excellence is a form of legalized theft whereby those who are less productive steal from those who are more productive. Changes in the legal requirements both for hiring references and for firing have fostered a civil service mentality in the private sector. Individuals need to be protected from capricious acts that threaten their livelihood; however, one of the most capricious acts is depriving individuals of their right to be rewarded based on what they produce.

4.6 *Recommendation: Preserve the right to an employment record.* As is commonly practiced, all employers would be required to conduct an annual or semiannual job performance appraisal for each employee. An appraisal form would be used to rate the employee's performance in all areas applicable to his position. In many occupations, peer review could be an important part of this appraisal. The appraisal form could have verbal comments, but the primary evaluation would be a numerical score in each category. Each company would set up an internal procedure to review evaluations deemed unfair by an employee, but by law, such proceedings would not be appealable to the civil courts. Within one month after the appraisals, the company would compile a statistical summary of the scores of all employees in each area rated. They would provide each employee with a copy of this summary and send a copy to the state employment office where it would become a public record.

Employment termination actions could be justified either on unusual special circumstances or on chronic poor job performance. Unusual circumstances would of course require special documentation. However, the job performance appraisal sheets would form the only admissible basis for chronic poor performance. In general, companies would be justified in firing an employee whose overall performance habitually fell in the lower ten percentile. Layoffs (where not preempted by seniority considerations, which I recommend abolishing in a later section) would be based on performance ratings, with no more than a twenty percentile difference allowed between the highest performing employee laid off and the lowest performing employee retained. When an employee left a company, the company would be required to retain his employment records for twenty years.

The performance appraisal forms would provide the only basis for past employment references. When an individual sought employment, he could authorize that only the dates of his past employment be released or he could authorize his former employer to send copies of his appraisals. Since the applicant would also have copies of his past appraisals, his authorization would by law release his former employer from any civil actions over the contents of the past appraisals. Employers would rightly be more cautious in hiring applicants who refused to release their former employment appraisals.

Holding Tank for Social Maturation

The role of providing a holding tank for social maturation is another important, but unacknowledged, function of formal education. Mankind's long period of adolescence is a biological adaptation of our species to allow for the extensive development of the human brain in response to education. While three-year-old horses run in the Kentucky Derby, a three-year-old human is far too immature socially and intellectually to function as an adult. Mercifully, our biology keeps children physically small and manageable until our brains have attained a reasonable level of development.

The time of puberty defines nature's selection of the period of adolescence. This selection is always a survival tradeoff between the advantages of complete development and the disadvantages of a longer period of dependency and vulnerability. The lesser amount of education required during humanity's early development and the comparatively short human lifespan favored a metamorphosis to physical adulthood at about thirteen years. However, humans at thirteen years of age are still socially immature.

The prosperity of human society required that young people be held in adolescence only until they became sufficiently mature to assume the responsibilities of adulthood. For the last few hundred years, the age of twenty-one years for legal majority has represented a social consensus on the period of adolescence required in civilized society. In rural communities, the children lived and worked on their parent's farms until they were socially mature enough to function as adults. When they reached social maturity (usually late teens for girls) and early twenties for boys, they got married and joined society as adults. In urban social settings, formal high school education ended at eighteen. However for boys, a four-year period in the army often provided the necessary bridge between adolescence and adulthood.

In modern society, the university experience provides a period for adolescents to break free of their home environment and achieve sufficient social maturity to function as adults. This important social role of universities in no way demeans their intellectual function. The focus of higher education must not be that you have to stay in school until you are twenty-two, but rather that you can only stay in school until you are twenty-two; because when you reach social maturity, society is going to throw you out in the real world and put you to work supporting yourself and contributing to the prosperity of society. Unfortunately, the social maturation role inevitably contributes to a holding-tank mentality that is responsible for much of the perceived irrelevance of both high school and university course material. Hopefully, the previous recommendations to promote a more objective career-focused educational system will also help restore a proper sense of urgency to the educational process.

Investment

Investment is the creation of tools to amplify human ability and thereby enhance future prosperity. The process of investment involves two steps. The first step is the diversion of current prosperity-producing efforts toward the creation of facilities or equipment that we expect to be useful in producing tomorrow's prosperity. The second step is the actual utilization of the new facilities and equipment to enhance future prosperity. An investment is considered to be prosperity enhancing or profitable if the cost in present wealth is less than the increase in time-discounted future wealth over the service life of the investment. Reaping the benefits of past investments is the easy part of investment. The hard part of investing is making the decision to invest current wealth and in so doing lose its contribution to current prosperity. Failure to adequately invest, as America is now doing, seriously diminishes America's potential for future prosperity.

Tools can be considered to be another class of living power structures. Tools are arrangements of matter created by living cells to enhance prosperity. Humanity's tools are really physical extensions of the human body that amplify our capabilities. The tusk of an elephant and the spear of a human both extend the capabilities of their respective living power structures. However, unlike the elephant, we can have a whole workbench of different tools each specialized for a particular use. While all our tools are presently inanimate, many are quite active and some can operate for considerable periods producing useful work without any human intervention.

The unique characteristic of tools is their complete obedience without any additional motivation or rewards. Mankind initially domesticated animals to enhance its prosperity both through animals' enhanced abilities (service) and by undercompensation for their efforts (predation). However, all but the least intelligent animals required motivation, which reduced their net output. Human slaves suffered from the same motivational requirements, which led to the invention of more sophisticated forms of feudalism. Tools, however, make perfect slaves. Tools do what they are told without seeking a free-market return for the value they add to the production process. Tools are such a powerful prosperity-enhancing mechanism, because humanity can claim both the productive output due to human effort and the productive output due to the tools, less any maintenance/depreciation requirements.

The current prosperity of mankind is largely due to the uncompensated productive effort of our tools. This book was created through a combination of my effort and the incredible support of my Macintosh computer. Without the enhanced efficiency of computer word processing, writing this book would have been considerably more time-consuming. Yet my computer has never asked for any share of the royalties, and it is perfectly content to support me for a few kilowatts of electricity. The dramatic ongoing revolution in workplace productivity due to the personal computer is only one example of the many ways in which human prosperity is supported by the undercompensation of technical servants we depend on to run our modern world. The dramatic advance of civilization over the last few hundred years was primarily driven by advances in the number and ability of our tools. Likewise, our hopes for enhanced future prosperity will be largely determined by the level of our technology as measured both by the number of our tools (investment) and by their increased productive ability (technical innovation).

From the dawn of civilization up to the industrial revolution, tools were universally viewed as beneficial to mankind. Since the ownership of tools was widespread throughout the population, so was the control over the tools' use and the distribution of the tools' productive efforts. Investment decisions such as "Should I build or buy a new plow?" were individual free-market decisions. Territorial feudalism enabled the feudal lord to steal the peasant's harvest, but the peasants still controlled the use of their simple tools. Technical innovations dramatically advanced the ability of tools to perform productive effort. This led to the industrial revolution, characterized by a rapid increase in the number and sophistication of mankind's tools.

The growth of industrial feudalism began the politicization of investment decisions. Territorial feudalism only required a mechanism of legalized theft to control the finite supply of land. However, unlike land, there is no inherent limit to the number of tools. Therefore, the past and present existence of industrial feudalism requires mechanisms of legalized theft to control capital investment in the production and utilization of tools. The birth of industrial feudalism was orchestrated by a class of tool owners (industrialists) who controlled both the ownership and use of society's tools. Control of society's tools gave the industrial feudal lords both the total return of the productive output of the tools and a greater than free-market return on the productive output of the workers whom they allowed to use the tools. This system of feudal theft led to the union movement to obtain higher compensation for workers' productive efforts. The compensation received was not based on contributed value, but simply on the relative political power of the unions and the industrialists. In many cases, the political power of the unions led to investment disincentives, directly due to overcompensation for workers' efforts and indirectly due to a tax policy that discouraged investment.

America has become a low investment, high consumption society. America's savings rate is among the lowest of the major industrialized nations, and our government's deficits further reduce capital available for productive investments. As a result, our infrastructure is falling into disrepair; and our industries are, in many cases, either underequipped or using obsolete equipment. This situation is seriously limiting America's prosperity today and, if not reversed, will even more seriously limit our future prosperity. America's low savings rate is primarily a reflection of the incentives for consumption and the lack of competing rewards for investment. The easy availability of credit encourages consumption and the double taxation of dividends and the capital gains taxation of inflationary gains are examples of two rules that discourage savings and investment.

Investment has become a class issue in American society. While the many instances of legalized theft in our society unfairly distort the income distribution in America, the highly skewed distribution of wealth is largely due to the unwillingness of most of the American people to save. The small percentage of Americans who do save end up owning most of our country's wealth. America's distorted wealth distribution both creates a power structure that facilitates legalized theft and makes most Americans envious of the wealthy few, even when they are not stealing. Since America's prosperity depends on increased investment, we must democratize the distribution of wealth by promoting savings to significantly broaden the American people's sense of ownership in their country.

Efforts to increase America's savings rate first require a better understanding of the factors that motivate people to save. I believe that there are at least four such motives, namely (1) rainy day security, (2) middle-age prosperity, (3) old age or retirement income, and (4) financial security for one's children.

Ironically, one of the primary causes of America's low savings rate is the success of our social institutions in creating a sense of security. Historically, rainy day (or, disaster) security was one of the primary motives for savings. Life was full of short-term problems ranging from illness to poor harvests. The daily experience of seeing the suffering of friends and neighbors who had not adequately saved to cover some emergency was a constant reminder of the need for rainy day savings. The periodic occurrence of war, depression, or natural disasters left whole generations traumatized into being confirmed savers. Scarlett's famous line in *Gone with the Wind,* "I'll never be hungry again," dramatically portrays the effects of disasters on people's savings habits.

The marvelous social innovation of insurance provides people with protection from many rainy day risks. Insurance substitutes the certainty of a small loss (the premium) for the uncertainty of a large loss. True disaster insurance (e.g., fire, flood, earthquake, etc.) promotes security without affecting savings, since most people would never save enough to cover such catastrophic losses. However, the pervasive use of insurance in America to cover events that are almost routine removes the need for each person to accumulate excess savings to independently cover such events.

Government social programs have carried the effects of insurance a step further. While insurance reduced the need for excess savings by pooling risks, insurance at least accumulated funds to cover losses before they occurred. Insurance companies accumulated reserves that were a source of investment capital. However, most government programs eliminate saving for emergencies by paying for disasters out of current taxes or by borrowing. With insurance, the individual was responsible for his own welfare, which fostered self-reliance and encouraged a rainy day savings mentality. With government programs, someone else does the disaster planning. The resulting cradle-to-grave security, while socially desirable, unfortunately discourages citizens from rainy day savings.

The savings motive to provide for middle-age prosperity is not, I believe, uniformly distributed throughout humanity. While

105

separating this motive from the others is difficult, there is a clear intellectual distinction. Each individual has a different time value of money, which may change with his age or circumstances. The prevailing interest rate in society is the weighted average of everyone's time value of money. If an individual is future oriented, then his time value of money will be less than the prevailing interest rate. Such individuals are motivated to consume less today and invest the rest at what to them seems like an attractive interest rate. Conversely, individuals who are strongly present oriented have a time value of money that exceeds the prevailing interest rate. These individuals are motivated to spend all they earn and even borrow against future income. We should be reluctant to place moral judgements on individuals' differing sense of the time value of money. While there is a moral responsibility to save for periods of hardship (either the unexpected hardships of middle age or the expected hardship of old age), there is no moral criterion to judge how an individual should distribute his available spending over his lifetime. However, the absence of moral judgement does not mean the absence of economic consequences.

The removal of rainy day saving through social innovations that promote security and thereby discourage saving is resulting in a more skewed distribution of wealth in America. This skewed distribution of wealth is leading to class distinctions based not on income differences but on wealth differences due to the accumulated savings difference between high– and low–interest rate people. Unfortunately, the power bestowed by wealth presents an irresistible temptation for the wealthy to bias society's rules to steal from the rest of society (right-wing theft). Similarly, the envy and legitimate anger of the rest of society tempts them to bias society's rules to steal the accumulated wealth of the savers (left-wing theft).

The total material wealth of America is simply the accumulated savings of the past and present members of our society. While the technical innovations that support this wealth are timeless, the actual material goods all depreciate in value due to wear and obsolescence. As a Boy Scout, I used to hike along the C&O Canal, north of Washington, D.C. While the locks still work after one hundred and fifty years, the canal today only contributes recreational value and a sense of history to our national prosperity. The advance of American prosperity—driven by technical innovations in transportation in the form of railroads, motor highways, and now air transportation—has completely depreciated the investment value of the C&O Canal. The technical innovations that describe these modern transportation systems made them possible, but only the savings of Americans made them happen. American prosperity depends on policies that encourage savings. America's growing national debt that is being acquired not to fight a war to preserve our freedom or to make capital investment, but simply to feed current consumption, is an example of negative savings that must be stopped to preserve the future prosperity of America.

4.7 Recommendation: Ratify a balanced budget amendment.
Recent history has conclusively shown that our government is unable to resist special interest pressures to steal from future generations through noninvestment deficit spending. I have joined the growing ranks of individuals who have concluded that a balanced budget amendment is the only way to stop this process.

Retirement income generates by far the biggest requirement for savings. While rainy day uncertainties may be more compelling, the magnitude of savings required to support retirement income far exceeds any rainy day situation. Because retirement income needs are uncertain, oversaving for retirement results in inherited wealth for future generations. For these two reasons—the magnitude of savings required for retirement and the significant potential for inherited wealth—retirement savings represent America's best opportunity for accumulating investment wealth needed for our national prosperity.

The Social Security program was a social innovation directed at providing a measure of retirement income security. The original program was intended to provide a small guaranteed retirement income based on a mandatory savings plan financed through payroll deductions. The original program was based on a trust fund that would be a source of national wealth accumulation, but could only pay retirees an amount based on a free-market return on their contributions. However, temptations for theft led to violating the trust fund, with severe consequences for American prosperity.

The rape of the Social Security system is likely one of the largest instances of legalized theft in American history. This rape of Social Security is allowing about two generations of retirees to receive benefits that are completely out of line with a free-market return on their contributions. The size of their payment is simply a reflection of their political power and the use of that power to commit left-wing theft. When given the choice between remaining with Social Security (with the implied promise that America's children would support them in their old age) and leaving the system (and taking their contributions and their employers' contributions with them), most workers would opt for the latter. The survival of the current system (which taxes many workers more than their federal income taxes) is a testament to both Americans' sincere compassion for their parents' generation's well-being and the awesome political clout of senior citizens where for many the size of their social security check is their only political issue.

The Social Security program is a disaster for American investment and the future prosperity of our country. Like the national debt, the Social Security program saddles tomorrow's workers without their consent with the burden of supporting their parents' generation in retirement. The existence of the Social Security program discourages today's income producers from saving for their retirement, and the burden of Social Security transfer payments makes any additional savings extremely difficult. Since the Social Security burden falls hardest on lower and middle income groups, these groups become nonparticipants in the wealth creation process. This leaves the already wealthy and the committed savers owning a progressively larger share of the smaller-than-it-should-be pie of America's wealth. Getting out of the Social Security mess and returning America's retirement savings to a trust fund basis is an essential objective for American investment and future American prosperity.

We need to institute by democratic consensus a Mandatory (individual) Asset Accumulation Program (MAAP). Such a program would accomplish several very important objectives. First, MAAP would require each American to accumulate sufficient wealth to provide adequate income for his/her retirement years. However, MAAP would also enhance American prosperity by (1) enhancing the savings rate and thereby promoting the accumulation of national wealth and (2) significantly democratizing the distribution of wealth in America and thereby promoting political support for proinvestment policies. There is, of course, no easy way out of Social Security. We have lost a generation of wealth accumulation due to the rape of the Social Security system. The millions of retirees on Social Security must be provided for while we return to a system based on individual accumulated assets.

4.8 *Recommendation: Institute a Mandatory (individual) Asset Accumulation Program (MAAP).*
In broad terms, a MAAP would use payroll deductions, supported by a schedule SE-type form, to deposit funds into individually managed retirement/savings accounts. The following paragraphs present a candidate program in more detail to better illustrate some of the features. The typical MAAP program shown in figure 4-1 is based on a real return of 6 percent after taxes and inflation. All four curves on this figure represent appreciation curves at 6 percent real return. The bottom or minimum, curve reaches a value of $250,000 at age sixty-five. At 6 percent, this would provide an income of $15,000 per year without drawing on principal. The upper three curves reach principal values of $350,000; $450,000; and $500,000 at age sixty-five that provide incomes of $21,000; $27,000; and $30,000. The four curves correspond to different levels of manda-

MANDATORY ASSET ACCUMULATION PLAN

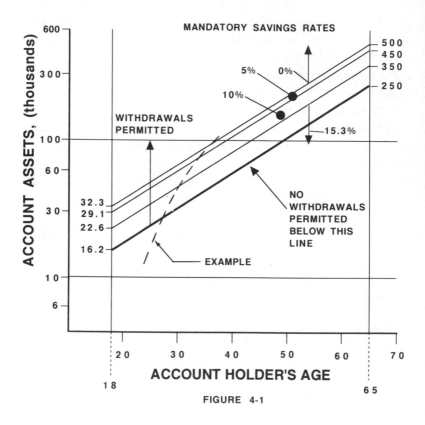

FIGURE 4-1

tory savings of 15.3 percent (current Social Security rate), 10 percent, 5 percent, and 0 percent.

The mechanics of MAAP administration would be through private financial institutions, much like Individual Retirement Accounts (IRAs). At the end of January, each taxpayer would receive both a statement of the net worth of his MAAP account and his W-2, showing both his wages and his income withholding that had been deposited in his MAAP account (initially 15.3 percent of his salary). Once the value of accumulated MAAP assets exceeded the minimum curve, the MAAP statement would start showing an accessible balance. This balance could be left in the MAAP account or withdrawn at the individual's discretion without any tax consequences. Individuals who left all or part of their balance intact would see their MAAP assets increase up to the second curve. When MAAP assets exceeded the second (or 10 percent) curve, the MAAP administrator would inform the customer's employer to only withhold 10 percent of salary for MAAP contributions. When the MAAP assets exceeded the third curve, withholding would drop to 5 percent; and finally, when the assets exceeded the top curve, no withholding would be required. If the assets fell below one of the asset accumulation curves due either to poor investment return or use of the assets, the appropriate withholding rate would be reinstated.

The following example shows the power of wealth accumulation at the 15.3 percent rate currently withheld for Social Security. This example is presented in table 4-1, and the MAAP assets are shown by the example line on figure 4-1. In this example, an individual starts working at age twenty-two at $25,000 per year and begins contributing to his MAAP at 15.3 percent per year. His salary increases by $1,500 per year up to $35,000 at age thirty. By age twenty-seven (after only six years on the program), his assets exceed the minimum curve and start creating an accessible balance. If he does not withdraw his accessible balance, in only three more years at age thirty, his assets exceed the second curve and his mandatory saving rate drops to 10 percent. During the first nine years, his annual contributions at 15.3 percent (current Social Security rate) range from $3,825 to $5,325. His account balance at the end of nine years is $51,894 and the accessible balance is $17,416.

CASE HISTORY EXAMPLE OF MAAP SAVINGS

AGE	SALARY	SAVINGS	INTEREST	TOTAL SAVINGS	ACCESSIBLE BALANCE
22	25,000	3,825		$3,825	
23	26,250	4,016	230	$8,071	
24	27,250	4,208	484	$12,762	
25	28,750	4,399	766	$17,926	
26	30,000	4,590	1,076	$23,526	
27	31,250	4,781	1,415	$29,789	$840

AFTER ONLY 6 YEARS, SAVINGS EXCEED MINIMUM CURVE
AND START CREATING AN ACCESSIBLE BALANCE

AGE	SALARY	SAVINGS	INTEREST	TOTAL SAVINGS	ACCESSIBLE BALANCE
28	32,500	4,973	1,787	$36,549	$5,864
29	33,750	5,164	2,193	$43,905	$11,379
30	35,000	5,325	2,634	$51,894	$17,416

AFTER 3 MORE YEARS, SAVINGS BALANCE EXCEEDS SECOND CURVE AND
MANDATORY SAVINGS RATE DROPS TO 10%

AGE	SALARY	SAVINGS	INTEREST	TOTAL SAVINGS	ACCESSIBLE BALANCE
31	36,000	3,600	3,114	$58,608	$22,061
32	37,000	3,700	3,516	$65,824	$27,085
33	38,000	3,800	3,949	$73,574	$32,510
34	39,000	3,900	4,414	$81,888	$38,360

AFTER ONLY 4 MORE YEARS, SAVINGS BALANCE EXCEEDS THIRD CURVE
AND MANDATORY SAVINGS RATE DROPS TO 5%

AGE	SALARY	SAVINGS	INTEREST	TOTAL SAVINGS	ACCESSIBLE BALANCE
35	40,000	2,000	4,913	$88,802	$42,662
36	41,000	2,050	5,324	$96,180	$47,273
37	42,000	2,100	5,771	**$104,051**	$52,209

AT AGE 37, AFTER ONLY 16 YEARS ON THE PROGRAM, THE SAVINGS
BALANCE EXCEEDS THE FOURTH CURVE. AS LONG AS THE SAVINGS GROW AT
6%, NO FURTHER CONTRIBUTIONS ARE REQUIRED AND THE BALANCE AT
AGE 65 WILL EQUAL OR EXCEED $500,000.

TABLE 4-1

Although the mandatory savings rate drops to 10 percent after age thirty, the combination of savings plus interest continues to rapidly build assets. After four more years, at age thirty-four, MAAP assets reach $81,888. This amount exceeds the third curve and permits savings to be reduced to only 5 percent. Even at 5 percent, at age thirty-seven (after sixteen years on the program), MAAP assets reach $104,051 and mandatory saving ceases. At 6 percent net return, this amount will reach $500,000 at age sixty-five and provide an annual income of $30,000 per year.

The continued ascent of man (driven by technical innovation and investment in tools that use new technology) makes the democratization of wealth through savings (such as MAAP) absolutely essential. The increasing ability of mankind's tools is unleashing a new social challenge. The term *automation* and the human concern it expresses arose when machines began to acquire the ability to perform highly skilled tasks with little or no human assistance. Prior to automation, the machine owners needed human labor to run the machines. The social threat of automation is that the machine owners can now create wealth with technical "servants" without the participation of large segments of society. Clearly, education is becoming more essential in the race to keep human workers in the production loop by increasing human ability. However, this is a race we are bound to lose as our tools become increasingly more sophisticated.

As our national income increases, a progressively larger share will be due to the productive efforts of our technical servants. Therefore, individual prosperity in the modern world will require both human ability (to produce wealth directly) and personal investment (to claim a share of the wealth produced by society's machines). A MAAP is needed to democratize the distribution of America's wealth. Without such democratization of wealth, income will also become hopelessly skewed and America will be polarized into a have/have-not society. The inevitable political struggles between the right-wing theft of those who own society's tools and the left-wing theft of those who do not will derail America's ascent toward an enlightened society based on freedom.

Innovation

Innovation is the only path to long-term future prosperity because innovation is forever. As discussed in chapter 1, education only lasts for the lifetime of an individual. Therefore, each generation must relearn the applicable skills of their parents. Investment may last longer, but it also depreciates and must be replaced. However, innovation is permanent because knowledge does not depreciate. The remarkable ascent of man has been driven by a multitude of social and recently technical innovations that have dramatically enhanced humanity's ability to work smarter and thereby to prosper. Social innovations were the key factor in mankind's early development and social innovations continue to play a vital role in future prosperity. All the recommendations in this book (including the ones in this chapter) are social innovations directed at enhancing American prosperity by improving the efficiency of our human interactions. While acknowledging the importance of social innovation, the rest of this chapter is specifically directed at technical innovation.

The diversity of American society and the individualism of American culture make technical innovation the strongest tire to carry us to the prosperity of an American renaissance. Unfortunately, American industry seems to be losing the innovative spirit that was such an important factor in the ascendancy of American technology during the last hundred years. The last half of the 1800s and the first half of this century saw a steady stream of American inventions. The creative genius of men like Edison and the Wright brothers revolutionized technology and enabled America to become the industrial leader of the world. These men and their ideas founded great industrial empires. However, the subsequent ownership by industrial empires and the U.S. government of these ideas and all future inventions of the engineers they employ has resulted in the feudalization of American technology.

The awesome power of technical innovation to enhance human ability is a threat to the prosperity of existing political power structures. Technical innovations can threaten investment in plant and equipment with obsolescence. Innovations can require different educational backgrounds and job skills that can threaten the careers of current workers. Finally, technical innovations can torpedo existing free-market control mechanisms based on proprietary methods or other feudal controls. The creation of the light bulb is an excellent example of this process. Thomas Edison's invention ushered in a new era of prosperity for mankind and simultaneously caused the extinction of the whale oil lamp industry. Machiavelli understood these human concerns over innovation when he wrote the following admonition to would-be inventors.

It must be remembered that there is nothing more difficult to plan, more doubtful of success, nor more dangerous to manage than the creation of a new system. For the initiator has the enmity of all who would profit by the preservation of the old institution and merely lukewarm defenders in those who would gain by the new ones.

The Prince (1513)

Machiavelli would be quite at home in the twentieth century. The nature of man hasn't changed in the last four hundred years nor in the last four thousand. The difference is not in human nature, but in the degree of freedom provided by the political systems people live under.

One of the most important tasks of an enlightened society is to promote innovation and protect innovators from the power of entrenched systems that will try to stifle their innovations before the free market has a chance to properly evaluate them. Technical innovation is a more fragile commodity than social innovation. We are all socially educated and able to formulate alternate approaches to social issues. However, technical innovation requires both creativity and sufficient technical training to understand the physical relationships involved before one has a chance at formulating innovative approaches. Therefore, only technically trained individuals in a society are able to contribute technical innovations and these fewer individuals are easier to control.

America was one of the first nations to formulate patent laws to encourage technical innovation. This favorable treatment of technical innovators was an important contributing factor to the flood of innovations that help propel American prosperity. However, like so many good intentions in our society, intellectual property laws have been subverted to promote the prosperity of American corporations rather than American society. Company ownership of employee patent rights is a nearly universal condition of employment. This absolute control, which allows companies to suppress any divergent technologies that emerge, has the terrible consequence of thoroughly discouraging technical creativity. One company I know goes so far as to require that each engineer submit at least one patent application a year in a desperate attempt to coerce creativity without the promise of any significant reward for creative effort.

The corporate ownership of employee patent rights is compounded by a dearth of opportunities for engineering self-employment. Freedom for engineering professionals strikes at the heart of the feudal control of American technology. Independent engineers would be able to apply some of their time toward inventing and developing new technologies in their field of expertise. These new technologies could threaten the market position of existing companies. The existence of an independent engineering employment option would also threaten corporate power structures by introducing more competition into engineering employment practices and benefits. Not surprisingly, the latest tax law revisions specifically tightened up on the requirements for self-employment of consulting engineers and computer specialists. The congressional intent to reinforce feudal control of American technology by large corporate and government agencies by stopping the hemorrhage of technical professionals to independent employment is painfully obvious.

The efforts of large corporate power structures to control technology in their areas of business goes beyond control of their employees to efforts to capture and suppress competing technology. Whereas Japanese companies often license new technology, American and European companies traditionally do not. A successful license gives a small company funds to continue innovating in the area of the license and also encourages other innovators to explore improvements in that area of technology. If companies do anything, they usually buy patents giving them complete control over the technology and its future development. Sometimes they do this to develop a new technology, but often they purchase a patent merely to suppress the technology if they feel it threatens their current business approach. Companies also hire experts in competing technology and fund their research for a sufficient period of time to establish control of the technology. If they then decide to suppress that technology, they offer the expert another position knowing that he can no longer independently pursue his invention.

The pervasive control of advanced technology by the federal government has suppressed innovation in the very areas that could propel American to technical leadership in the twenty-first century. There is no better example of this process than the record of America's space program. Americans should be proud of the continuing accomplishments of the brave men and women who are leading our space program. However on an absolute scale, the accomplishments of the last twenty years are anemic compared to the accomplishments of the preceding fifteen years. After the national humiliation of the first Vanguard attempt, President Kennedy turned America's technical professionals loose on the seemingly impossible task of manned exploration of the moon in less than ten years. The decade of the sixties saw a phenomenally rapid series of accomplishments leading to the Apollo 11 lunar landing in July 1969. This initial landing was followed in the next few years by a series of even more spectacular manned lunar landings and the flight of Skylab, America's first space station. These technical accomplishments were paralleled by a wealth of scientific data from both manned and unmanned explorations. The subsequent redirection of national resources away from space redistributed space program employment in the private sector, but failed to comparably trim the government support structure. Today, twenty years later, we have no launch system that can compare to either the payload capability or the per pound launch cost of the Saturn V developed in the 1960s. We have no Quonset hut operational space station like Skylab, because we are busy designing a gold-plated Taj Mahal. However, we do have a billion-dollar space telescope with incorrectly focused mirrors.

Rather than being a facilitator for space exploration and space science, the U.S. space program is in many ways a choke point for these activities. Space program funds are allocated to big program projects, because these are the only activities that can justify the government bureaucracy and the private sector bureaucracies that support it. The political power of these expenditures in local economies insulates the system from any attempts to reform it. Therefore, we continue to spend considerable resources on space with comparatively little output for our investment.

Americans love innovations that make their lives easier and more prosperous. That is why we love our Japanese cameras, TVs, and cars. They offer well-engineered innovations and quality products. Our newspapers are full of soul-searching articles over the apparent demise of Yankee ingenuity. However, Yankee ingenuity was always motivated by Yankee profitability. The men and women who created the great technical innovations that propelled America to world leadership took great pride in the contribution they were making to America. However, their primary motivation was their own prosperity.

Engineering in America is no longer a profession, but simply an entry level job. With no possibility of remuneration for technical innovation, management is the only avenue for career advancement. The result of this system is a bloated bureaucracy of technical managers attempting to obtain prosperity through people skills for which they were neither trained nor especially gifted, rather than using the technical skills in which they were trained and which America so desperately needs.

Japan is a nation of engineers while America is becoming a nation of attorneys. A recent newspaper article noted that Japan has four hundred engineers per ten thousand people, while the United States has seventy. Sixty-five percent of Japanese company directors have engineering degrees while in the United States 65 percent have degrees in law, accounting, or finance. We have no reason to blame the fine men and women who choose law, accounting, or finance for a career. Americans still have the freedom to choose their careers and that choice is strongly influenced by the financial rewards they expect to receive. In every society human resources flow to the highest return. However, in a free society the highest return is also the highest value as determined by a free market. There are no long-term shortages in a free market. Consequently, the widespread public concern over America's technical competitiveness in world markets and the dominance of U.S. patent applications by foreign inventors are irrefutable evidence of the feudalization of American technology, which diverts wealth from the scientists and engineers who create technology to the power structures that control technology.

The control of American technology is based on laws that both deny American engineers a share in the inventions they create and also deny them the opportunity for self-employment and the chance to independently develop new technology and new products. The attorneys who are hired to support this system for the most part do not understand technology and therefore are not in a position to contribute to the creation of new technology. However, they do understand the law and how the law can be used to control existing

119

technology and thwart the development of new technologies that might threaten the commercial positions of the companies they work for. The impressive amount of new technology that America does produce is primarily due to the efforts of companies that are small enough to remain entrepreneurial and fortunate enough to have remained independent of large company control.

America's large companies and government laboratories are vast technical collective farms where our scientists and engineers toil as serfs for the power structures. Just like in the former Soviet Union, they produce output; but like all collective efforts requiring individual initiative, their output is a poor return on the resources invested. However, every American who receives new product catalogues knows that innovation is not dead in America, it is simply being redirected.

American is still full of creative men and women trying to enhance their prosperity by inventing new and useful products for American society. However, the laws of our land deny them any intellectual property rights in the area of their employment (which of course is also the area of their primary expertise). Therefore, these resourceful Americans invent new products for the home and garden: new lawn sprinklers, new automatic pet feeders, new swimming pool toys, etc. Like their counterparts in the former Soviet Union, these Americans cultivate the small private plots they are allowed to till and in general produce a bountiful harvest. However, the Soviet Union couldn't feed its people from private plots and American industry can't maintain world leadership on home-and-garden innovation. While American innovators apply their talents at the fringe of society, the core of American industry is rotting away from obsolescence. Most of the better engineers in large companies have escaped to management and many of the rest are struggling to get there.

4.9 *Recommendation: Establish an inventor's bill of rights.*
We need an inventor's bill of rights to guarantee inventors a reason-

able share of the results of their creativity as an incentive for American innovation. Certainly companies, who employ engineers, and the U.S. government, when it funds programs, deserve the lion's share of the return on new innovations. However, a guaranteed return to the inventor is the crucial element needed as an incentive in the process. An example of such a plan might be as follows.

Employee inventors would be guaranteed 10 percent of the value added to products containing their patentable inventions. Value added would be based on the value in the market place of a comparable product without the innovation, less the production cost of including the innovation. If the innovation was created under a government contract both the company and the inventor would be guaranteed 10 percent (for a total of 20 percent) for the life of the patent. In general if the work was performed under a subcontract, the contracting company or the government would receive the 80 percent share and the subcontracting company and inventor would each receive 10 percent. Invention compensation payments would be independent of the employee's normal pay and even independent of his employment.

The ability to obtain compensation for technical innovation would motivate many of America's technically creative men and women to remain in technical work. While their salaries might not compete with management, the sum of their salaries and invention compensation could provide them with a comparable total income. This would open the door for many less creative but bright and competent technical professionals to become managers. Many of these men and women have better people skills and would make better managers than their more creative coworkers.

4.10 *Recommendation: Require development or licensing of new technology.*
The purpose of intellectual property laws is to promote technical innovation by giving the inventor certain exclusive rights to the invention for a limited period of time. These laws were never intended to be used to give political power structures the right to

suppress technology. Therefore, the patent laws should be changed to require development or licensing of all patented inventions. The annual patent fees, which only serve to force small inventors to sell to companies, are no financial burden to a large company wishing to suppress a technology. Under this recommendation, any individual or corporation could file a request for a 5 percent nonexclusive license to commercialize any existing patent. If the current holder of the patent was failing to make reasonable progress in commercializing the invention, the government could authorize the requested licenses. Reasonable progress would be based on both the size of the company holding the patent and the importance of the invention.

4.11 *Recommendation: Establish a narrower definition of proprietary information and trade secrets.*
The patent laws provide seventeen years of protection for inventions made public through the patent process. However, companies can choose not to file for patents and keep the technical details of their processes proprietary. If these companies are powerful enough, they can keep these processes proprietary forever and thereby gain a perpetual patent right. A good example is soft drink formulas. In this age of detailed drug testing and DNA mapping, I find it hard to believe that one could not fairly easily determine and reproduce the formulas for Coca-Cola, Pepsi, and all the other soft drinks. However, the burden of proof would be on the inventor to show that he did not steal the formula. Without unlimited resources, the inventor would simply be crushed by the legal forces of these large companies. Society benefits from the open format of the patent process both by ensuring that new technology will pass into the public domain in seventeen years and by promoting the synergistic development of technology through the public description of patented innovations. The laws protecting nonpatented proprietary material should be changed to limit the period of this protection. Companies would be allowed to protect nonpatented concepts or processes for a period of only five years. After five years' time, this material would be considered to be public domain.

4.12 *Recommendation: Promotion of small business opportunities in engineering and science.*

One of the greatest benefits of freedom is the diffusion of power. A free market is the diffusion of economic power to the people. Democracy is the diffusion of political power to the people. We need a similar mechanism to diffuse technical power more broadly throughout American society. My recommendation is that all government contracts require that 20 percent of the research and engineering expenditures be subcontracted to small businesses. The government monitors of such public fund expenditures would have review and approval rights on these subcontracts to ensure the wide dispersal of technical knowledge and expertise throughout American society.

Our American renaissance depends on maximizing the strengths of the American people. Our strength does not lie in raw numbers; other nations have far more people than we do. Our strength does not lie in organization; other nations, like Japan, are far more ordered and disciplined than we are. America's strength lies in the creative individualism of the American people. America is a diverse society formed by immigrants from many lands. These immigrants were risk-takers willing to leave their homes to make a better life in a new land and willing to work hard to make their dreams a reality. Over the last two hundred years, their descendants have produced a series of political, social, economic, and technical innovations unprecedented in human history. These advances were fueled by the freedom of American society, which both fostered motivation and encouraged ability enhancements—especially innovation. The restoration of freedom from theft to American society, particularly in the area of technical innovation, can unleash the creative talents of the American people and propel our nation into the twenty-first century on the crest of an American renaissance.

5 / Rebuilding the Road to Prosperity

The Failure of American Government

The failure of American government to adequately serve the interests of our country is the leading cause both for the explosive growth of legalized theft in America and for America's failure to achieve the level of prosperity that our great country is capable of. There is an emerging consensus that government is directed at serving special interests by enabling their schemes of legalized theft, rather than directed at serving the broad interests of the American people. This section supports that consensus and seeks both understandings and recommendations to redirect American government to enhance American prosperity. However, this effort needs to be conducted with the full awareness that government is a thoroughly political institution and the purpose of all political power structures is to promote the prosperity of a group of individuals, often at the expense of the prosperity of the larger interest of humanity. Nations exist to promote the interests of their people; political parties, corporations, unions, professional associations, etc., all exist primarily to promote the interests of their members. These political power structures, like the organs of the body, can significantly enhance society's prosperity as well as their own through their directed specialized talent. However, political power structures need to be continually watched and redirected to prevent them from turning cancerous and becoming parasitic on society.

Government in a social power structure serves some of the same functions as the brain serves in biological power structures.

124

In an ant colony, the queen provides rigid central control over the activities of the nest. As discussed previously, this emphasis on order promotes today's prosperity at the expense of innovation, which is necessary for tomorrow's prosperity. As a result, all higher animals have adopted a looser social structure to allow the species to improve through biological innovation resulting in differential prosperity and survival of individual members of the group (i.e., survival of the fittest). The evolution of mankind toward complex social interactions created a command and control dilemma in the human social power structure. During our early history, mankind regressed to a centralized authoritarian command structure. This provided the order needed to focus social efforts and allowed the rulers leisure time to innovate for the benefit of all. However, increasing human prosperity resulting from accumulating social and technical innovations led to a parasitic ruling class. The ascent of enlightenment, which reached its fullest expression to date in the ideals of America, offers the opportunity to bring evolution full circle. An enlightened society strives to maximize individual liberty and reward individuals based on their production valued by a free market. Such a society achieves both the altruism needed to provide order while also maximizing the opportunities for social and technical innovation.

In an enlightened society, government defines and enforces the rules that both encourage and—when necessary—restrain self-directed individual human behavior to operate in the best interests of society. Our founding fathers understood the command and control dilemma of humanity and developed a system of government with limited powers and a myriad of checks and balances. American history has been a constant process of testing this system as people and their political power structures sought to circumvent social constraints to profit at others' expense. The explosive rise of technology has given rise first to industrial feudalism and then to professional feudalism. These new schemes of legalized theft are analogous to the mutant strains of virus that invade our bodies. A period of time is required for the body to recognize the invaders and to develop antibodies to repel the attack. During this delay, the toxins of the invaders produce a period of sickness when the body is functioning below par.

American history contains many periods of sickness caused by the mutant schemes of theft of our own political power structures or those of other nations. We are currently in one such period of sickness. We have successfully recovered in the past by invoking the ideals of human liberty expressed through responsible democratic process. This process requires understanding the pathology of the disease and then having the courage to take the actions needed for a successful recovery.

Representative democracy is the diffusion of political power to the people, with that power expressed through their elected representatives. This marvelous social innovation seeks to achieve the efficiency of centralized control while preventing tyranny through popular control of the elected representatives. However, this system only works when the representatives act in the interests of the people they were elected to represent. Our representatives are human beings motivated first by their own prosperity. Many, I honestly believe, are also motivated by a sincere desire to promote American prosperity. When personal interests and national interests are in conflict, they may sometimes act in the national interest. However, they are not saints and we cannot base a successful system on the expectation that people will routinely behave against their self-interest. The challenge with government, as with all political institutions, is to devise a set of rules and incentives so that serving personal interests also serves America's interests.

The failure of American government is both a reflection of the divergence of societal and personal interests, and the increasing importance of government in American society. Corruption has always been a part of politics and from an historical view today's members of Congress are angels compared to many of the senators and representatives during the Grant administration. However, in those days the role of the federal government was much smaller, and their greater corruption had a relatively insignificant effect on our country. The pervasive role of government in modern American society requires that government operate much more efficiently than it has in the past. While limiting the role of government is part of the answer, anarchy is not the road to an American renaissance. Our increasingly complex society requires a strong and responsive government. I believe achieving a more responsive government will require both changes to make our elected representatives more responsive and changes to increase the role of the American people in the political process.

The only effective control that the American people have on government policy is through the election process. Therefore, we should examine this process both for the causes of our current problems and for changes that will improve our representation.

The unwillingness of the American people to support the political process with their vote and with their money is the primary cause of America's political problems. In all fairness, this situation has been fostered by elements in our society who do not want popular control. However, as long as we have the right to vote, we have nobody to blame for the current situation but ourselves. The right to vote is the cornerstone of democracy, yet in a many elections fewer than half the eligible voters participate. This public apathy accentuates the power of special interests. We need to change the election process to encourage greater voter participation and provide a clearer verdict of voter sentiment.

Many voters are unhappy with the system and do not feel they are adequately informed of their representative's or candidate's stand on important issues. This is not surprising since politicians avoid taking stands on controversial issues. Since we are more sensitive to what we don't like than to what we do, we are more likely to remember when we disagree with a candidate than when we agree with him or her. Therefore taking stands on important issues loses votes unless the stand is relatively noncontroversial.

Candidates understand this negative bias in the electorate and orient their campaigns toward discrediting their opponents rather than presenting their own views on key issues.

5.1 *Recommendation: Require issue statements.*
Each candidate for federal, state, or local office would be required to submit three positions requiring a yes/no vote. Each candidate would be required to vote on the issues he submitted as well as on those submitted by other candidates. The candidate could include a short paragraph on each issue explaining his position, but could not refer to other candidates or their positions. This material would be provided to each voter with their voter pamphlet. Voters could judge the candidates based on the seriousness of the issues they raised and by their response to all the issues.

A common excuse voters offer for not voting is that they do not support any of the candidates or that their vote is simply a vote against the other candidate(s). The election process should provide voters with the opportunity to express these sentiments as a means to send a clearer message to both elected and defeated candidates.

5.2 *Recommendation: Institute a negative voting option.*
For each office the voter could express both positive and negative votes as follows.

Candidate A	**Support** ☐
	Lesser Evil ☐
Candidate B	**Support** ☐
	Lesser Evil ☐

None of the Above .... ☐

Lesser-evil voting would permit voters to make their position known to both candidates without throwing their votes away. The electorate could decide to use these votes in a variety of ways.

1. Split votes could be merely informative, with the plurality candidate being elected. OR
2. If "None of the Above" received a plurality, a reelection would be required with different candidates. AND/OR
3. If the plurality candidate received a majority of his votes from "lesser evil," a reelection would be required with the parties allowed to run the same or different candidates.

The dependency of our elected officials on special-interest contributions for campaign financing is the major cause of special-interest control of American government. If America's low voter participation is embarrassing, our political contribution participation is scandalous. A recent article on campaign costs stated that a successful US Senate campaign required about $8 million in an average state and up to $20 million in a large state like California. These amounts are both astronomical compared to a senator's salary and minuscule on a per voter basis. For example, with about twenty million eligible voters in California, four Senate campaigns (e.g., two for each major party) every six years is only (4 x $20M)/(6 x 20M) = $0.67 per voter per year. Our unwillingness to support the political process by even this minuscule amount forces our elected officials to prostitute themselves to special interests for the funds to get elected. This incredible shortsightedness costs us each thousands of dollars, with the savings and loan crisis being only the latest example.

The limited income tax deduction for campaign contributions was an excellent program for broadening the popular funding base of political campaigns. I have to be suspicious that the repeal of this law was influenced by special interests' desire to tighten their control of government.

5.3 Recommendation: Restore a limited campaign contribution deduction.
Restore and enhance the limited income tax deduction for political

contributions by allowing a 75 percent direct tax credit for contributions up to $100 per couple ($50 for single returns), doubling this amount in election years. At the same time, prevent fraudulent use of this deduction by requiring political groups to report contributions and by checking this item on a significant number of the returns filed. Impose a penalty of ten times any amounts fraudulently claimed.

The issue of term limits for elected officials requires a tradeoff of the real benefits of continuity of leadership versus the penalties of political corruption and lack of social innovation. Continuity of leadership and the positive feedback of reelection are compelling reasons to allow elected officials to be permitted to stand for reelection and to serve a reasonable time in the same office. However, the old saying that "power corrupts and absolute power corrupts absolutely" expresses a nearly universal weakness in our human nature. Only rarely do we find individuals who are able to resist the temptation to use power to improve their position at others' expense. Since both the temptation to abuse power and the ability to do so increase with time in office, the time-proven solution (from the consuls of Rome to the president of the United States) is to limit the term of elected officials.

The most compelling reason for term limits is not the visible corruption of political dynasties but their intellectual stagnation, which thwarts social innovation. While the human mind has an amazing capacity to grow and adapt, we are all fundamentally products of our early experiences. Political leadership, whether by kings or by elected representatives, inevitably follows the biological model of innovation. The new leader brings innovative ideas that promote prosperity by allowing the society to work more efficiently. While enlightened leaders continue to provide a few new ideas, a periodic change in leadership is the only proven way to ensure truly effective social innovation.

Term limits can provide the opportunities for fresh, socially innovative leadership without losing the accumulated experience of former political leaders. There are many positions in government, industry, and universities that can enable former political leaders and their advisors to continue to use their talents and experience. While society needs to monitor this process to prevent "revolving door" abuses, this intellectual cross-fertilization can have a very beneficial effect on American prosperity.

5.4 Recommendation: Establish term limits for elected officials.
All elected offices should have term limits. These limits should be selected to balance the advantages of continuity of leadership with the disadvantages of corruption and lack of social innovation. When conditions warrant, the electorate can modify term limits to better balance these conflicting objectives.

We need more democracy in our republic. Our political system is gridlocked on many important social issues. I believe that more direct voter participation is the only way to permit meaningful social innovation to relieve the current paralysis. While the recommendations previously presented in this section should improve the accountability of our elected officials, even their implementation is highly unlikely without at least the threat of direct voter intervention. Meaningful reform on such issues as gun control, the criminal justice system, welfare, education, drugs, abortion, taxation, environmental issues, government entitlement programs, government spending, professional feudalism, intellectual property, and many other pressing issues is simply not possible solely through the representative process. On all these issues our elected officials face entrenched minorities who have the power to wreck the careers of anyone who opposes them. Only through popular votes (or the threat of such votes) can governmental policy (i.e., the rules of our society) be made to reflect the will of the American people.

A recent national survey on abortion makes the need for increased democracy in America perfectly clear. The survey reported that 71 percent supported the current *Roe v. Wade* limits on abortion and 88 percent would favor allowing abortions in cases of rape or incest. However, feelings on the abortion issue are so strong that 42 percent of the voters would oppose a candidate who opposed their stand on abortion *even if the candidate agreed with them on all other issues.* Not surprisingly, the abortion issue paralyzed Congress and led to the absurd situation in 1973 of nine learned men on the Supreme Court attempting to address this issue. The Supreme Court is a marvelous institution for addressing complex constitutional issues. However, abortion is a moral issue that doesn't require a Ph.D. in law. The profound issues of what limits our society should place on abortion should be decided by a popular vote of the American people. My personal preference would be for a national law that set upper and lower limits on abortion by popular vote. For example, the American people might decide to prohibit third trimester abortions except to save the life of the mother as an upper limit and to prohibit restrictions on the sale of birth control devices as a lower limit. The individual states would then be empowered to set their own limits (within the national range) by popular vote to account for regional differences of opinion on this very important moral issue.

5.5 *Recommendation: Expand democratic expression.*
There should be the opportunity for an expansion of popular vote decisions in American society. The following are some recommended guidelines for this process.

1. Where: at all levels of government, from city/county to national.
2. Qualification for ballot initiative
   a. Thirty percent of legislative body (i.e., city council or US Senate).
   b. Voter petition with 5 percent of registered voters.
   c. Voter application with supporting polls. The traditional petition process is both too cumbersome and time consuming, and not indicative of widespread voter support. There are many competent polling companies who could be li-

censed to conduct polls to qualify issues for public vote. A citizens' group wishing to qualify an initiative would fund a licensed polling company to conduct a poll on their issue. Such a poll showing evidence that at least half the voters favored an issue would be sufficient to qualify that issue for popular vote.

This recommendation to use polls to place issues before the voters drew a negative response from several of my reviewers. They cited the volatility of public opinion and noted that slanted wording could significantly bias the results of the poll. I concur that a public agency should review the wording of proposed initiatives for distorted language before polling the people's opinion. However, I remain a strong supporter of polls as a timely and inexpensive means to obtain popular referendums on positions that have demonstrated popular support.

3. Timing: much more frequently to allow a more timely response to the will of the people. As a suggestion, hold elections within the times stated below following the receipt of a qualifying poll on an issue.

	Federal (months)	State (days)	Local (days)
Poll with over 50% favoring	6	90	60
Poll with over 2/3 favoring	3	60	30

4. Winning Requirement: no decision if fewer than 50 percent of eligible voters vote. Winning requires 60 percent of those voting in state and local elections. In federal elections 60 percent nationally and a majority in two-thirds of the states. This requirement for a supermajority on popular referendums is based on the conviction that our representative government should still define most of the rules of society. Popular votes should be reserved for issues where a clear preponderance of the people favor a position, but they have been unable to obtain government action through the representative process.

5. Method: allow voting by mail, by phone with suitable verifica-

tion (e.g., PIN numbers) to control fraud, and possibly by using automated teller machines at commercial banks.
6. Issue limitation: no more than three issues at each election, with priority determined by highest poll value. Any bumped issues would be decided at another election in thirty days.
7. Proportional voting: proportional voting would be required whenever the issue could be so formulated. For example, instead of "Shall the state be authorized to purchase $300M of school bonds," the ballot would read:

School bond authorization	($)	Example results (%)
	0	20
	100M	20
	200M	35
	300M	25

In the example shown, only 25 percent of the voters approved $300 million, 60 percent (i.e., 35% + 20% in the above example) approved at least $200 million, and 80 percent (more than a two-thirds majority) approved at least $100 million. Therefore, a school bond authorization of $100 million would be approved; the voters have been given a real choice in directing government expenditures and the school board has been given a message on the level of expenditures that the public wants to support.

The direct intervention of government in economic activity creates a basic conflict of interest. The fundamental purpose of government is to define the rules that direct social behavior. We have a legislative branch to define the rules, an executive branch to administer the rules, and a judicial branch to adjudicate disputes. This arm's length objectivity is shattered when government also plays the game using the rules it has created. The table below and the text that follows contrast three areas of government that involve both direct government activity and supervised government activity.

Direct Government Activity	Supervised Government Activity
• US military	• US military contracts
• NASA	• NASA contracts
• Public transit	• FAA

The U.S. armed forces are the largest single direct government activity. While some of the criticism directed at our armed forces for bureaucracy is justified, for their size I believe the U.S. military is by far the most efficient and cost-effective operation of American government. Much of the credit for this efficiency is due to the enlightened actions of U.S. military leaders to privatize as much of the operation as possible. For example, the U.S. Air Force operates its planes and missiles, but they do not design and build them. This delegation of function to the private sector allows both for free-market competition (sometimes compromised by political pressure) to obtain the best equipment and, more importantly, for the flexibility to allow private sector resources supporting military operations to rise and fall. Military bases are a classic example of the inflexible bureaucracy created by direct government activity. Even when the military wants to close a base, Congress (who writes the rules) intervenes in the execution of those rules.

The National Aeronautics and Space Administration (NASA) is, I believe, an unfortunate example of the overextension of direct government activity. The Apollo Program led to the allocation of extensive private resources to the space program and the creation of many NASA facilities both to supervise these activities and in many cases to perform the activities. After the moon landings, America decided to reduce space expenditures and private sector resources were redirected. However, the civil service structures could not be as easily redirected. To my knowledge, no NASA center was ever closed; in fact, this bureaucracy has continued to grow. The fault is not with the people. From personal experience, I can attest that the vast majority of these men and women are bright, hardworking, and dedicated Americans. The problem is with the system of direct government activity that inflexibly allocates both human and material resources.

The Federal Aviation Administration (FAA) is a good example of a successful government-supervised activity. The private sector designs, builds, and operates the nation's airplanes. However, the FAA plays a vital supervisory role in both licensing the planes and their pilots, and in operating the airways. While our air transportation system is also far from perfect, its successful operation contrasts sharply with the mess experienced by many of our public transit systems. Public transit systems exist because some elements of society want to provide a service that the people who use the system are either unwilling or (they would say) unable to pay for. Such a service could best be provided by a competitive contract to the private sector together with whatever level of subsidy is socially desired. However, this arrangement makes visible the transfer of wealth from those who don't use the service to those who do. Direct government operation both hides the magnitude of fare subsidy theft from the electorate and creates a bloated bureaucracy to operate the system.

Ownership and the rewards that go with it are inseparably linked with the motivation to incur risk. When the decision-makers in any organization are unable to benefit from the rewards for successfully incurred risks, the system becomes noninnovative and bureaucratic. I am indebted to a retired air force colonel who took me aside and explained the birds and bees of bureaucracy. The way it works, he said, was: "One 'I got you' is worth ten 'at a boys.' If you take some risk and do a good job, the system says 'at a boy.' If you do this four or five more times, you get more pats on the back. However, if you screw up even once, you're dead meat. Therefore, the way to survive in a bureaucracy is to do nothing (or more realistically, as little as possible), because if you do nothing you can do nothing wrong." Fortunately, this man and many others I have known were willing to ignore this advice and take risks for American prosperity. However, the larger the company and the further removed the decision-makers are from ownership, the less incentive there is for risk-taking. Government is, of course, the extreme example of the separation of risk and reward. When your salary is determined by time in grade, and risks only mean the opportunity for termination, bureaucracy is the predictable result. The many fine men and women in government service are not bureaucrats. They are simply intelligent human beings who work for their own prosperity by playing by the rules that society has laid down for them.

5.6 Recommendation: Privatize government services.
The solution to government bureaucracy is to privatize government services to the greatest extent possible. The example of the U.S. Armed Forces provides an excellent example of the successful implementation of this approach. Civil servants would provide an administrative core that would direct government efforts by defining, awarding, and administering contracts to private sector companies. Like military service, civil service should be based on a twenty-year service life with a partial pension allowing the retiree to have a second career in the private sector. Only the key managers would continue to work beyond their twenty years. This would keep the civil service flexible and minimize the growth of government bureaucracies. The partial civil service pensions after twenty years of service should not be considered a retirement, but only a partial compensation for a forced career change.

The Social Diseconomies of Scale, Part I—Industrial Feudalism

The objective of all living power structures is to enhance the prosperity of their members through cooperative association. Biological power structures are cooperative associations of cells. Social power structures are cooperative associations of plants or animals, primarily competing against other species. Political power structures are subunits within social power structures. Political power structures seek prosperity through specialization, which benefits them and the larger society they are a part of. However, political power structures also seek prosperity through controls that enable them to steal (i.e., transfer resources at less than free-market value) from the other members of society. Unfortunately, these two prosperity mechanisms exist concurrently. Fortunately, the socially beneficial economies of scale diminish with size while the social diseconomies of scale usually increase with size. Therefore, the overall prosperity of society is best served by closely monitoring the activities of all political power structures within society and by controlling their size to achieve the best balance between their positive economies of scale and their predatory diseconomies of scale. The failure of the American people to control the size of the political power structures in our country has permitted many of these institutions to become parasitic. The fault is not with these institutions or the people in them, but with the failure of society to properly control their size and direction.

Size and the power imbalance that goes with it are the basic enabling mechanisms for all forms of feudalism. Slavery was sustained by the power of the state, primarily through naked force of arms. However, as civilization advanced, mankind learned to use the mantle of law as a cover for feudal theft. The territorial feudalism of the Middle Ages was legitimized by an array of civil and religious laws but was ultimately sustained through superior force. With the advent of democracy (diffusion of political power to the people), the magnitude of feudal theft has become limited by a combination of the size imbalances of the political power structures in society and by the apathy of the people to their victimization by legalized theft. Over the last two centuries, mankind has battled the rise of industrial feudalism (use of the control of the means of industrial production to distort the free market for labor, capital, and industrial products) primarily through laws that attempt to compensate for size imbalances, rather than by taking direct action to correct size imbalances. However, the record of history shows that the vast array of laws and regulations directed at preventing the abuse of industrial power for legalized theft have not been nearly as effective as the periodic restructuring of industrial empires to reduce their size and power advantage and thereby restore competition.

The concept of free competition requires that the participants be of roughly equal size and ability. In wrestling matches the participants are grouped by weight and in team sports the teams are often grouped by ability. Where competition between unequal contestants is required, society can make some compensations. For example, we handicap horses by adding weight and we handicap golfers by subtracting some strokes. However, social systems have difficulty maintaining free competition when large discrepancies in size or abilities exist. I remember one of my grade school math textbooks had a picture of two cavemen negotiating the price of arrowheads. One caveman with a deer on his shoulder had three fingers raised while the other caveman sitting on the ground making arrowheads had two fingers raised. We assumed this was a free-market negotiation only because the cavemen were of equal size and neither had a weapon present.

The basis of capitalism is the formation of political power structures consisting of the owners of material resources who apply those resources to enhance their own prosperity. Their prosperity depends on their ability to obtain as high a price as possible for the goods or services they provide and to pay as little as possible for inputs required. When conducted within the framework of a free market, capitalism is an efficient allocator of resources and a marvelous engine for human prosperity. The problems that arise in capitalist systems are not the fault of the system, but of size and, therefore, power imbalances among the participants. Big organizations subvert the free market in two important ways: Big organizations create power imbalances between the participants in the production process that invite control for the purpose of theft, and big organizations also reduce the number of players and thereby reduce free competition in the marketplace.

The competition between employers (and their delegated managers) and nonmanagement employees is one of the most fundamental conflicts in civilized society. Typically, the employer provides most of the investment needed to manufacture a product or provide a service that he hopes society will find more valuable than the resources required to create it. This investment can include land, buildings, and equipment. The employer typically also provides leadership and assumes the risk for the venture. The employees provide the motivation and ability to use the resources provided by the employer to accomplish the desired task. The primary source of conflict is the allocation of payment received for the service among the participants. Unfortunately, there are no good solutions for size imbalances in labor-market competition. As long as large companies exist, there will be the need for large unions (with all their problems) to protect employee interests.

The competition among suppliers for the public's business is the basis of a free-market economy. Although individual consumers are much smaller in size than the corporations that act as production units, a free market is maintained by (a) the consumer's repeated ability to choose between several suppliers and (b) the free flow of capital, which permits other suppliers to join markets with above average return and thereby increase competition. As the size of a company increases, free-market competition decreases both because the consumer is offered fewer choices and because the higher market entry costs discourage new producers.

Reduced innovation is a nearly universal consequence of large-company control of a market. While large companies may remain efficient at producing today's products, like the biological model they often react very negatively to new ideas that may involve risk or require capital investment. The failure of American consumer electronics companies to replace their vacuum tubes with transistors due to their investment in vacuum tube technology was a major factor in their demise and the dominance of Japan in consumer electronics. The lesson America's large companies learned from this experience was not the need to innovate, but the need to control the ownership of new ideas to prevent others from disrupting the market through innovation. The control of electric automobile technology by the automotive industry and the control of solar energy technology by the fossil fuel industry are two examples of new technologies whose development is being thwarted by existing companies at the expense of America's prosperity. This issue of intellectual property control was previously discussed in chapter 4.

Many large companies exist not to serve their stockholders and certainly not to serve the public, but simply to promote the power and prosperity of their rulers. When viewed in the pragmatic context of human history presented in this book, this statement is neither surprising nor particularly appalling. The separation of ownership from the control of operation means that salary (direct compensation) and power (indirect compensation) are the only rewards available to corporate management. While many companies base executive salary partially on profit, the primary basis for salary and the perks of power is the size of the company, not its profitability. Not surprisingly, this incentive system has resulted in many vast corporate conglomerates. These corporations often employ some of America's brightest business and technical talent. However, in many cases, these corporations are neither leaders in stockholder return on investment nor are they leaders in producing innovative new products in their respective fields. Therefore, these companies are inefficient users of both human and capital resources and, as such, neither serve their stockholders nor American society.

White-collar bureaucracy both in private industry and in government is likely the largest instance of right-wing theft in American society. Like upper management, middle management is rewarded based on the size of the corporate empire, usually meas-

141

ured by the number of employees. Therefore, empire building is the proven technique for growing the ranks of management. Blue-collar featherbedding is blatant, but at least it is honest. Putting a fireman aboard a diesel locomotive is an inefficient, but not totally wasted use of one person's talent. (The fireman gives the engineer an extra pair of eyes.) Such featherbedding increases the number of workers, but not the number of locomotives. By comparison, white-collar bureaucracy is carefully disguised by make-work activities that leave the extra workers and managers busy doing work of little economic value. Unfortunately, this make-work often requires additional resources like computers, support staff, travel, etc., that further adds to the cost of bureaucracy. Company size and lack of management ownership both strongly favor bureaucracy. Increasing size complicates upper management's task and lack of ownership diminishes upper management's incentive for controlling bureaucracy.

Division is the natural response of biological and social power structures to excess size. Amoebas grow and divide. Animals and plants reproduce. Beehives swarm. Since these power structures are based on altruism, division occurs when such division is in the best interests of the system. However, because human political power structures exist for the prosperity of their rulers, they continue to grow far beyond the optimum size for social prosperity. From the political empires of old to the economic empires of today, society needs to take the initiative to divide political power structures when their size no longer serves the best interests of society. When this policy is applied to corporations, a key objective should be to enhance the shareholder's equity by restructuring the corporation for more efficient and more profitable operation.

5.7 Recommendation: Control corporate size.
The antitrust laws should be expanded to allow for the evaluation of large corporations and the ordered breakup of those deemed to

be too large and socially inefficient. The criteria for this evaluation should be as follows.

1. Size—The absolute size of a company is one of the best indicators of the tendency for bureaucracy, lack of innovation, and inefficiency. Therefore, company size is the most compelling justification for dividing the company into smaller corporate units.
2. Dominance in Key Markets—This classic antitrust criterion, which has been gutted in recent years, should be reinvigorated and used to divide dominant companies to ensure competition in the market.
3. Profitability—Profitability (over a period of years) is the best measure of return on society's financial and human resources. Large companies that retain vigor by achieving profitability (through efficient operation, not by control of the market) in excess of their industry's average should be encouraged to continue without restructuring.
4. New Products—Companies that are more innovative than average should also be assessed favorably.
5. Capital Requirements—Some industries have larger capital requirements that socially justify a larger corporate structure.
6. Other Factors—Factors such as convictions for law violations (e.g., fixing contracts, pollution violations, regulatory violations, etc.) should also be considered as a basis for restructuring.

The demise of capitalism in America is a major cause of many of the socially diseconomic practices of large corporations. True capitalism is the ownership of the means of production, not its delegated control. Henry Ford was a capitalist because he owned the Ford Motor Company. Today's CEOs are not capitalists, they are simply highly paid overseers. For readers who may have watched the TV program "Alien Nation," I mean nothing sinister by the word "overseer." These are honest, hardworking men and women who direct their efforts toward promoting their own prosperity. We labor under a myth that people work for companies. They never have and they never will. People work for themselves. Is there a single vice president of a Fortune 500 company who wouldn't jump ship tomorrow if offered the position of CEO of his company's competitor? There is nothing illegal implied here. We need not imply that our VP would steal any secrets from his former employer. He would simply apply his talents in a free market to obtain the best return.

Companies run by nonowning managers suffer from the same problems as representative government, discussed in a previous chapter. The managers only pursue the interests of the shareholders when the rules of the system create a common interest. However, shareholders do not elect corporate officers and therefore have no direct control over the actions of the managers of their company. Shareholders only elect members to the board of directors, but members of the board of directors are often nominated by management, which is a blatant conflict of interest. Every year my alma mater sends me a ballot giving me the opportunity to vote for members of the university's board of directors. Each director presents a position statement and there is usually a choice to vote for five out of ten candidates. By contrast, corporate elections are typically one-party slates with only the option to withhold one's vote.

5.8 Recommendation: Institute contested elections for corporate board of directors.
For each publicly held corporation in the United States, 50 percent of the board shall stand for reelection each year. The slate shall include at least three candidates for every two open positions. Each candidate shall present a statement of his or her qualifications and views to the stockholders. Contested elections are a time-proven technique for flushing out dirty laundry and promoting innovation.

We have term limits for president (and hopefully we will eventually have term limits for other elected offices). However, corporate management is more like a feudal fief where people hold office as long as they can control the power. While nepotism is rare, corporate officers often play the dominant role in picking their successors. The issue of term limits for corporate officers involves the same tradeoffs discussed previously for government office, namely, continuity of leadership versus corruption and lack of innovation. I believe the conclusion reached for government office holds just as well for corporate officers.

5.9 Recommendation: Establish term limits for corporate officers.
For all publicly held corporations in the United States, the maximum term of the chief executive officer would be limited to eight years.

There is no better proof of the unresponsiveness of many companies to the interests of their stockholders than the outrageous compensation packages of many American corporate executives. However, the current public moralizing against these men and women over their pay is as pathetic as was President Kennedy's jawboning of the steel industry to reduce its prices. In a free country and a free market, there is nothing wrong with asking for as much as you can, because in a free market you will only receive what you are worth. The fact that we don't see many of these highly paid executives being stolen by their competitors is a clue that they are being paid more than they are worth. A CEO has every right to ask for a $4 million salary, but it shouldn't be his handpicked board of directors' sole decision to grant it.

5.10 Recommendation: Stockholders must approve CEO's salary.
For all publicly held corporations in the U.S., the concurrence of a majority of the stockholders shall be required for all increases in the total compensation of the highest paid corporate officer. This compensation increase shall first be approved by the board of directors. All directors who approved the increase shall be noted with an asterisk on the proxy. For example, a corporate proxy ballot might read:

1. Directors: Brown, Green*, Jones*, Smith*, and White
2. President's Total Compensation: increase from $1.8M to $2.5M.
   (Directors with * voted for this increase.)

Reducing the number of large corporations in America (where such restructuring promotes long-term stockholder equity) and making corporate management more responsive to stockholder interests will increase corporate competition in America. However, these actions do not address two other needs: (1) the need to promote greater profit sharing in American industry, and (2) the need to enhance the other end of the industrial spectrum comprising small businesses and self-employed individuals.

While profit-sharing agreements exist in many American companies, the preference of the owners of capital is to maximize the leverage of their capital to maximize their own prosperity. However, this policy both demotivates workers and fuels the growing class division in America between those who benefit a lot from investment and those who benefit very little. This resentment fuels social policies like double taxation of dividends that inhibit American investment. America needs both greater incentives for investment and greater sharing of the risks and rewards of ownership.

5.11 *Recommendation: Institute tax-favored profit sharing.*
Companies would be encouraged to institute profit-sharing plans by being allowed to deduct a dollar from their taxable investment profits for each incremental dollar of profit sharing paid to employees. For example, if an employee has a base salary of $30,000 and, due to the company's profit-sharing plan, in a good year the employee received $31,000, then both the $1,000 in profit paid to the employee and an additional $1,000 of profit paid to the stockholders (either as dividends or retained earnings) would be exempt from federal taxes.

Small privately owned businesses, which are the basis of capitalism, should be encouraged to promote American prosperity. While government and medium-sized corporations with nonowning management are necessary to support the large integrated products of modern society, expanded opportunities for small businesses and professional self-employment will enhance both the motivation and ability of American workers to create today's prosperity and, just as important, enhance the innovative ability of American workers to promote tomorrow's prosperity. Every study shows that small businesses are the most productive and account for a disproportionate share of the new jobs created. Like home ownership, business ownership gives individuals a greater sense of common interest in society.

The make or buy decision is one of the key decisions every company continually faces with both products and services. This decision should be based only on economics. Unfortunately, the bureaucracy factor favors the make decision, leading to overgrown and inefficient corporate structures. Like my previous recommendation to privatize the government, we also need to privatize business.

5.12 *Recommendation: Subcontract tax incentive.*
All businesses would be permitted to deduct for federal tax purposes 110 percent of the expenses paid to other companies for goods and services related to their line of business. For example, a car company could not claim the extra 10 percent for electric power or copy machine purchases. However, the company could claim the additional 10 percent for a wide variety of support services (e.g., accounting, legal, medical, maintenance, management services, engineering design, research, etc.), as well as for components that it could have reasonably manufactured in-house.

This tax benefit to businesses to stay smaller would more than pay for itself through increased efficiency in the American economy. Companies would retain their essential core but would be motivated to shed noncore services to companies that specialize in that area. The expanded opportunities for small business and professional self-employment would increase the base of ownership in America, leading to enhancement in both motivation and innovation in our society.

The Social Diseconomies of Scale, Part II—Professional Feudalism

The complexities of modern civilization are increasingly leading to human resource specialization, which has given rise to professional feudalism. The preceding chapter dealt with industrial feudalism and the ways in which control of the means of industrial production can be used to subvert the free market and steal from the other members of American society (by obtaining a higher return than would exist in a free market). The rise of industrialization makes human labor a smaller component in the total production of national wealth. However, the increasing specialization of labor reduces competition and enhances the opportunity for professional feudal theft through the control of human labor.

Fundamentally, professional feudalism is the control of the supply of labor to inflate its return above free-market value. Three approaches are used to accomplish this objective: (1) high entry costs, (2) direct entry controls, and (3) required procedures that inefficiently use human resources. The political power structures that engage in professional feudalism for the prosperity of their members perpetrate theft on the rest of American society.

Professional feudalism completely pervades American society. Virtually every profession or interest has been successful in instituting some practice that distorts the free market for their benefit. Attempting to remove every such feudal practice would be hopelessly idealistic and unnecessary, because many of these practices are not significant impediments to the free market. However, there are a great many major instances of professional feudalism that are having a serious impact on American prosperity. In most cases, the political power structures that perpetuate these feudal thefts also provide valuable benefits. As stated before, the fault is not with these organizations or with the people in them. Political power structures are by definition directed at promoting the prosperity of their members. The American people are responsible for controlling theft by political power structures in our society. The widespread existence of professional feudalism in America is simply evidence of our failure to meet that social responsibility.

Government is the facilitator of professional feudalism, just like all other forms of feudal theft in society. Government makes the rules that direct social behavior. The absence of rules to restrict feudal theft and, in many instances, the existence of rules that promote feudal theft are further evidence that government is not responsive to the interests of the American people. Therefore, as stated in the Declaration of Independence, it is the right (and duty) of the American people to alter the system. As previously discussed, the failure of American citizens to financially support the political process has forced our representatives to prostitute themselves to special interests to obtain financing for reelection. While I am hopeful that reforms can make the representative process more responsive to the interests of American society for normal daily operations, I feel more democratic participation of the American people is needed to resolve the major issues facing our society.

The pervasive nature of professional feudalism in American society could easily justify an entire book. My purpose here is simply to highlight several key examples. The following text briefly discusses these examples and their impact on American society and then presents recommendations for improvement. Hopefully this assessment will act as a catalyst for additional discussion, recommendations, and popular action to reduce the intolerable level of professional feudal theft in America.

The Accounting Profession

The accounting profession is an example of a combination of industrial and professional feudalism that constrains the earnings of many accounting professionals below free-market value. The certified public accountant (CPA) license is the control mechanism for the accounting profession. The CPA is socially justified as a mechanism to ensure that those individuals who perform accounting services for the public are professionally qualified. However, an opinion voiced by some who have taken the CPA exam (and passed) is that the exam is not a good discriminator of accounting ability, but merely an exercise in memorization. Whether or not this position is justified, the record shows that only a small percentage of college graduates in accounting go on to become CPAs. Therefore, the CPA license functions as an effective means to control the supply of accounting professionals allowed to work independently. Control of the supply of accountants able to work independently reduces the earnings of the vast majority of accounting professionals without CPA licenses and inflates the earnings of both companies that employ accounting professionals (industrial feudalism) and those individuals who are CPAs (professional feudalism).

Society places no professional requirements on individuals who perform accounting services as employees. While most companies hire individuals with a college degree in accounting to perform their accounting work, employers are free to hire anyone they wish to perform any accounting or bookkeeping functions as employees. This freedom extends even to very small businesses whose owners are not accountants and therefore not in a position to professionally judge the competence of those who do their accounting work.

Experience indicates that this completely unrestrained free market for employee accounting services works most of the time. For the most part, employers are smart enough to evaluate prospective accounting personnel based on their education and experience.

However, there are enough problems that if government were really interested in the public interest, there would be some minimal credentials for employee accounting services. The absence of any requirements on employee accounting personnel exposes the hypocrisy of the system. Employers don't want any restrictions on whom they can use to perform accounting work (which might raise their costs for accounting labor). However, they enthusiastically support restrictions that prevent college-graduate accountants from working independently without first obtaining a very demanding CPA license. This complete freedom for employers coupled with serious market restrictions on accountants creates a nice little system of industrial feudalism that enriches industry at the expense of Americans who work in accounting.

The growth of corporate accounting bureaucracies is part of the price America is paying for feudal control of the accounting profession. Since accountants cannot earn free-market wages for performing accounting services, the path to prosperity for bright accountants is to become a manager of those providing accounting services. However, managers require empires to manage and empires require justification. The multitude of accounting procedures in most American corporations provides an ever-expanding justification for more accounting services and more accounting managers to supervise these services. Like all corporate bureaucracies, the accounting bureaucracies are difficult to control because they are directed at promoting the prosperity of those they serve. The previous recommendations to downsize corporations and provide tax incentives for subcontract work will help constrain the explosive growth of make-work financial activities in corporate America. However, the success of these recommendations will be greatly enhanced by expanding self-employment opportunities for accounting professionals.

CPA firms exist both to provide independent auditing services to all sizes of businesses and to provide accounting services to small- and medium-sized companies and individuals who do not

151

require full-time accounting support. These firms must be run by a CPA, although the work can be performed by accounting professionals without CPA licenses. In fact, there are no professional requirements placed on the individuals performing the work as long as the work is performed under the authority and hopefully under the direction of the CPA. The CPA firms serve as apprenticeship programs since audit experience is required to obtain a CPA license. Unfortunately, this monopoly over the ability to perform audits and therefore provide audit experience gives CPA firms powerful control over their employees wishing to become CPAs. Not surprisingly, this control is often used to depress the wages of the employees of CPA firms and inflate the return paid to the CPA partners. Again, the fault is not with the people, but with a system of feudal control that allows some to steal from others.

The CPA is an example of the single-level credential abuse that also supports professional feudal theft in the medical, legal, and educational professions. The CPA should be retained as a top-level qualification for accounting professionals performing audits. However, college graduate accountants should, after a few years' experience, be allowed to routinely become licensed to perform nonaudit accounting services for the public.

5.13 Recommendation: Institute a licensed public accountant credential.

Institute a new accounting credential of Licensed Public Accountant. This license would require completion of a comprehensive program of college-level course work in accounting (i.e., bachelor of science or equivalent), plus five years of related work experience. The LPA license would allow an individual to perform all public accounting functions except company audits. The LPA would provide the public with assurance of professional standards, since either unethical or unprofessional shortcomings could result in the suspension or revocation of the LPA license. The LPA would provide the public and small businesses with an adequate accounting credential for normal accounting work. For unusually complicated accounting problems or audits, they could consult a CPA.

The Medical Profession

The medical profession is one of the clearest examples of professional feudalism in America. Medicine is both a highly skilled profession and one that literally has a life-and-death impact on society. The importance of health and well-being to human prosperity creates an irresistible temptation to try to control the market for medical services. Medical professionals are both some of the most capable and highly educated members of American society and, as individuals, some of the most compassionate and altruistic. The contrast between the altruistic nature of doctors and the professional feudal control of the medical profession is the most dramatic contrast I am aware of in our society. Of all the professional services, medicine is one of the most valuable and in a free market would reward its members with a generous return for their labor. However, the medical profession has used its power to institute controls over the practice of medicine in America that steal from the American people through an undersupply and therefore an overpricing of medical care.

The medical profession's control of the supply of health care in America is based on the control of the license that society requires for an individual to practice medicine. In theory, society through government actions should determine this licensing process. However, in practice, the medical profession has obtained complete control over determining who can practice medicine; and the awesome political power of the American Medical Association ensures that no elected representative will seriously oppose the AMA's usurped authority. The abuse of the licensing process manifests itself both in restrictions on the number of people who can become doctors of medicine and, more importantly, in the requirements to practice medicine.

The academic requirements for entry to US medical schools have reached the point of absurdity. While candidates for a doctorate in medicine should be selected from the top 5 to 10 percent of the student population, there is no excuse for requirements so severe that only the class valedictorian gets admitted to medical school. The reason, of course, is not the qualifications needed to become a doctor of medicine. The reason is the shortage of openings in US medical schools, engineered by the medical profession to control the supply of doctors and thereby inflate the cost of medical services above the free-market value. This has created a situation where doctors from major European nations with medical systems every bit as advanced as ours are clamoring to practice medicine in America. The system has also managed to thwart this attempt to restore a free-market balance to the supply of medical services in America. There is one entry point through the US Armed Forces that has enabled many qualified (but not superhuman) men and women to become doctors. Since many of these doctors remain in military service for their twenty-year retirement, this additional supply does not begin to rectify the shortage of doctors in private practice. A logical solution to the shortage of doctors would be to allow more qualified individuals to become doctors by (1) building more medical schools and (2) removing restraints on qualified foreign doctors. However, I believe the more immediate solution is to reform the requirements to practice medicine.

The single-level license to practice medicine is the primary cause of the inflated cost of medical services in America. Consider for comparison the automobile industry. Medicine deals with life and death, but you also trust your life to the mechanic who repairs your brakes and steering system. The relatively free market in the automotive industry has created dozens of job classifications. Each position requires a different degree of education and experience, from the assistant mechanic who checks your oil to the Ph.D.

engineer who uses computer simulation to design new cars for crashworthiness. Many of these positions either require a license or certification of special training. When the public needs automotive service, they can take their car to the individual who is properly qualified (but not overqualified) to perform the service they need. They do not call a Ph.D. engineer or scientist when they have a dead battery, they call the American Automobile Association for emergency road service. They call the AAA because the "Doctor" wouldn't make a house call, and even if he did the AAA can adequately handle the job for a lot less money.

The single medical license system in America creates a great void in the delivery of medical services. When Americans have a minor medical problem, such as a cold or flu, their only choices are to treat themselves with a medical encyclopedia and over-the-counter medicines or to go to a doctor of medicine. There are no individuals with bachelors' or master's degrees who are allowed to independently practice medicine. Fortunately, however, there are thousands of such qualified individuals in America: the registered nurses. These women and men work as serfs for doctors or hospitals because they are not allowed by law to offer their services directly to the public.

5.14 *Recommendation: Establish licensed medical practitioners (LMP).*

Permit registered nurses to set up private practices for providing medical services to the public. While the definition of these services needs detailed study, I believe they could include routine medical exams, vaccinations, treatment for colds and flu, treatment for minor injuries, and especially home visits. The LMP would be responsible for referring patients to specialists (i.e., doctors of medicine) and would be licensed to admit patients directly to hospitals. LMPs could work directly for hospitals and perform work on their own authority or, like doctors, they could have their own practice and work part-time in hospitals caring for their patients.

155

Opening the medical field to independent LMPs should go a long way toward mitigating professional feudalism in medicine. LMPs would take over most of the routine medical work, thereby giving the public increased access to medical care at far less cost. Small communities currently without a doctor could easily afford an LMP. Doctors' services would be reserved for care that required their greater knowledge and training. Doctor fees would likely remain respectable in recognition of the significant value of their services. However, the LMPs would substantially relieve the doctor shortage and likely bring frcc-market pressures to bear on doctor fees. After about ten years when the dust has settled on the introduction of LMPs, the public should reassess the need to further expand the supply of doctors.

The Legal Profession

The entire rationale for forming social power structures is the ability of individual biological power structures to work more efficiently together in a group. As discussed in previous chapters, this requires a set of behaviors (or rules) that efficiently organize group activities and a command and control structure that directs these behaviors.

Social laws are powerful tools for prosperity, but they also hold the potential for abuse. In lower animals, the behaviors needed for both individual and group interaction are encoded in the DNA as instinct. This process of instinctive behavior provides for consistent group action. However, the consistency of instinctive behavior opens the opportunity for abuse by any power structure that can use group adherence to a behavior to its own advantage. For example, over time bees evolved the behavior to swarm at the smell of smoke to preserve the hive in the event of a forest fire. Mankind uses his knowledge of this behavior to steal the bee's honey, by first filling the hive with smoke. This abuse of the rule of law creates a

156

conflict in bee behavior. If they evolve with a less automatic response to fire, they will be less susceptible to theft of their honey, but more susceptible to destruction by fire. The abuse of the rule of law in human society often has a similar disruptive effect that far exceeds the value of the stolen honey.

The legal profession has the responsibility of being the architect of the rule of law in human society. Throughout history, the power that flows from this extremely important duty has been used for the benefit of human society. Our Declaration of Independence, Constitution, and Bill of Rights are examples of the use of law and legal opinion to articulate social objectives and define rules for their execution. However, the power of law has also been widely used to create immoral systems of legalized theft. The legal profession usually receives the criticism for the abuse of law and often receives little praise for the positive role of law in promoting an orderly functioning society.

The blame for the many abuses of the power of law by the legal profession rests with the American people for our failure and the failure of our representative government to restrain these abuses. Lawyers and the legal profession are simply a political power structure in human society that exists primarily to promote the prosperity of its members. The task before us is to understand the abuses that exist, develop social innovations to minimize these abuses, and then through the power of representative government or direct popular initiative reform the rules of the system. The following paragraphs attempt to make a start at developing further understandings and recommendations in three key areas: (1) the criminal justice system, (2) the civil justice system, and (3) the legal requirement to practice law.

The criminal justice system in America has become inefficient and bureaucratic through the single-minded pursuit of the ideal of justice. The statue of justice with her balance and blindfold is a powerful symbol of the fairness and equality of treatment that we want our legal system to aspire to. However, all human objectives involve tradeoffs. Our obsession with justice at any cost has led to a criminal justice system with so many procedures, delays, and appeals that trial costs can run into millions of dollars. This outrageous direct cost is amplified by the indirect cost to society caused by the inability of the criminal justice system to timely process and convict those who violate the law. The issue facing the American people is the amount of money they wish to spend to provide those accused of breaking the law with a fair trial. The men and women who run the criminal justice system are human beings whose self-interest is served by making the process as complicated and costly as possible. However, society's interests would be better served by imposing a budget on the legal process. Nobody wants to see an individual falsely convicted of a crime. However, if the penalty for a crime is one year in jail, we shouldn't spend ten employee years of legal resources on the trial.

5.15 *Recommendation: Impose budgets for criminal justice procedures.*

The American people should impose budgets on criminal justice procedures. The budget should represent a reasonable expenditure of society's resources to provide a fair trial consistent with the punishment that society imposes for that particular crime. The judge would, of course, have discretion to exceed or underrun the budget for a given trial. However, the court costs averaged over the last ten trials would have to adhere to the approved budget. The criminal justice system, with the assistance of new laws or popular initiatives as required, would have to revise court procedures to conduct trials within the budgeted amounts.

The rest of the world looks at the U.S. civil justice system with amazement and disbelief. We are the most sue-happy country on earth. This situation is not the result of a larger number of socially unjust acts in our country, but of a civil justice system that financially rewards the redress of social grievances through the civil courts. More pointedly, this situation is the result of a civil justice system that offers lavish financial rewards to the legal profession for the attempted redress of grievances through the civil courts. In many cases, the civil suit is nothing more than legalized theft, with obstetric medical malpractice and minor automobile accident suits being good examples. When a baby is born in less than perfect health, we look for someone to blame and more importantly for someone with money to pay for the costs for additional medical care. Maybe new parents should carry insurance for handicapped babies. Maybe society should provide more support to such parents. But using the civil justice system to steal from doctors and their insurance companies to provide for such care is a miscarriage of justice. Minor traffic accidents are another burden on our civil courts. While automobile accidents are a legitimate source of loss, the proliferation of automobile accident suits is driven by the potential for a financial windfall that far exceeds the actual loss incurred.

The present civil justice system is a source of disunity in American society. We need a system that can provide prompt and fair adjudication of civil conflicts in society. However, the present system is both too slow for prompt redress of grievances and often excessively generous in awards. While many reforms have been proposed, few have been enacted due to the power of the legal profession to block changes that reduce their feudal control over the legal system. There is no point in blaming the legal profession for pursuing their own self-interest, because that's only human. Since most politicians are lawyers, reform of this political power structure will only come when the American people institute changes through popular initiative.

From my perspective there are two systematic flaws with the current civil justice system. The first flaw is in asking a jury without any professional training or experience to determine damages. This system often leads to awards based on emotion and not on a sound assessment of the actual damages. The second flaw is the winner-take-all methodology of the civil justice system, which is an unfortunate carryover from criminal proceedings. In a criminal proceeding, a defendant must be judged guilty or innocent. However, very few civil proceedings are completely one-sided. There are either two injured parties or one of the parties has some extenuating circumstances. Therefore, the requirement to either find totally for the defendant or the plaintiff is illogical.

5.16 *Recommendation: Incorporate professional damage assessment and fractional blame judgements in civil proceedings.*

The first phase of any civil proceeding would be to establish the value of the civil damages involved for both the plaintiff and the defendant. These costs would be established by court staff personnel and approved by a judge based on evidence presented by the participants. This professional assessment of damages, including pain and suffering, would provide a fair and consistent assessment of damages. Following this initial damage assessment phase, the participants could decide either to reach an out-of-court settlement or to proceed with a civil trial.

The second, or trial, phase of any civil proceeding would be to establish fractional blame and court-mandated payment of damages. By law, trials for damages below a certain level would be before a judge. Jury trials would be reserved for cases with more substantial damages, but both parties could still agree to a nonjury trial. After hearing the testimony, the judge or jury would assess the fractional blame of the defendant on a scale of 0 to 100 percent. In a jury trial, the jurors would each cast a ballot in the jury room with their assessment of blame and then discuss the results. After the discussion, the jury could revote. When at least half the jury agreed that sufficient discussion had occurred to resolve differences between the jurors, a final vote would be taken, averaged, and presented to the court.

The civil damages awarded by a trial would be based on the previously determined damages of the plaintiff and defendant, plus their court costs and the fractional blame assessment of the court. For example, if the averaged vote of the jury (or the judge) decided that the defendant was 70 percent to blame, this would also mean that the plaintiff was 30 percent to blame. In this example the defendant would be required to pay 70 percent (i.e., his assessed fractional blame) of the plaintiff's damages and the plaintiff would be required to pay 30 percent (i.e., his assessed fractional blame) of the defendant's damages. The net payment or award to each party would be the difference between these two amounts. For example, assume the plaintiff's damages were $100,000 and his court costs were $20,000, for a total of $120,000. Also assume the defendant had damages of $10,000 and court costs of $30,000, for a total of $40,000.

For this example the table below presents the judgement assigned to each party as a function of the jury's fractional assessment of blame.

Jury's Judgement of Defendant's Blame (%)	Defendant Pays ($)	Plaintiff Pays ($)	Net Award to Plaintiff ($)
100	120,000	0	120,000
90	108,000	4,000	104,000
80	96,000	8,000	88,000
70	84,000	12,000	72,000
60	72,000	16,000	56,000
50	60,000	20,000	40,000
40	48,000	24,000	24,000
30	36,000	28,000	8,000
20	24,000	32,000	-8,000
10	12,000	36,000	-24,000
0	0	40,000	-40,000

A civil justice system that included professional damage assessment and fractional blame judgement would be both a fairer system in terms of awards and a much less highly leveraged system. With the current system, the attorney's skill is highly leveraged, because a small difference in presenting the case can spell the

161

difference between getting a full award and getting nothing. With a fractional blame system, the facts would tend to speak for themselves. Certainly a better attorney could obtain a somewhat higher award, but the incremental increase might not justify the additional legal fees. Similarly, there would be less incentive to beat a case to death for a few extra percentage points in assigned blame. This would tend to speed up trials and also reduce legal costs. However, the biggest benefit of the recommended system would be a reduction in the number of civil trials. Since the damages would be determined before the trial and a trial could no longer offer an all-or-nothing verdict, the cost tradeoff between going to trial and settling out of court would more strongly favor an out-of-court settlement that is fair to both parties.

As with medical care, the single legal license system in America creates a great void in the delivery of legal services. When Americans have a minor legal problem such as a will, a small contract, or even a divorce or bankruptcy, their only choices are to be their own lawyers, using a bookstore guide, or go to a high-priced attorney. As with medicine, this practice is blatant professional feudalism whose only purpose is to restrict the supply of legal services to the American public for the enrichment of the legal profession. A Ph.D. in law may be socially justified for a criminal trial lawyer. However, there is no reason why competent men and women should not be able to earn bachelor's and master's degrees in law and be able to provide a lesser range of legal services to the public.

5.17 *Recommendation: License legal consultants.*
Universities should be permitted to offer undergraduate bachelor's and master's degrees in law. Graduates would obtain proficiency in certain aspects of the law, such as wills and estate planning, contracts, patents, divorces, etc. Upon graduation, the holders of such degrees would be able to apply for a license as a Legal Consultant. This license would permit the holder to offer legal services to the public in the areas of their specialties.

The Seniority System

The seniority system is such an important and pervasive form of professional feudal control that it deserves a separate discussion. This system is simply a system of feudal control whereby the older members of society who control the system steal from the younger members of society. This statement is in no way intended to demean the value of experience. Experience means enhanced ability obtained through the educational system of life. This enhanced ability enables an experienced individual to work smarter, be more productive, and therefore be more valuable. The agrarian model of a free market ("As ye sow, so shall ye reap") rewards experience, but has no provision for seniority. We expect a farmer with twenty years' experience to achieve higher yields than a new farmer. However, the corn doesn't care about the farmer's age, it only cares about the farmer's ability and motivation.

Seniority is often justified on the basis of need, much like Communism was. We reject the Communist approach of "to each according to his need," because Communism does not promote prosperity. Even theoretically applied Communism removes the incentive for expending anything other than minimum effort. Like all systems of theft, Communism broke down as people lost respect for the system. We are guilty of the highest hypocrisy when we condemn the Communist system (which nominally distributes resources based on need), while we condone the pervasive systems of seniority in America that blatantly distribute resources, based not even on age, but simply on the number of years in a specific power structure.

There are many other moral justifications used to legitimize the seniority system. We hear statements like, "You have to pay your dues." Have you ever noticed that those who want you to pay your dues are also the ones who collect the dues? We hear statements like, "Older workers have families with children to support." If an older worker is married and supports children, he can file a joint tax return, he can claim exemptions for his children, and he can deduct the interest and property taxes on his house. These are all incentives that society provides to encourage family responsibility. We are perfectly capable of providing whatever socially beneficial incentives the American people desire. However, using family values as a justification for seniority is simply a smoke screen for a system of feudal control and theft that has nothing to do with the social objectives it claims to support.

The areas of American society where seniority has the strongest hold—namely government, industrial unions, and education— are the areas that lag in productivity growth. Like Communism, seniority discourages both motivation and ability improvements. Younger workers have no incentive to either work harder or to improve their abilities so they can work smarter, because their rewards will come only with age. Similarly, experienced workers have no incentive to work harder or to use their experience to work smarter to justify their higher return, because that return is guaranteed by their age. In the nonseniority segments of American society, those who apply for a new job and those who seek promotion in their existing jobs must compete on the basis of their motivation and ability. These are the only objective measures of their potential to contribute to prosperity and therefore the only rational standards for determining their return in a free market.

5.18 Recommendation: Abolish seniority discrimination.
The laws of the United States should specifically prohibit any form of discrimination purely on the basis of age or number of years in a particular job or occupation. This should not be in any way construed to interfere with legitimate distinctions based on ability differences obtained through experience. However, these distinctions should be based on objective measures of job performance, not simply on time in grade.

164

The Educational System

The educational system is in many respects a cornerstone of advanced civilization. Since the vast part of human ability is now taught, the operation and even the survival of human civilization depend on teaching each new generation the skills they need to produce society's prosperity. However, education is also a leader in creating new knowledge and as such plays a vital role in supporting both social and technical innovations that enhance future prosperity. The vital importance of education as a tire of prosperity was discussed in chapter 4. The discussion in the following paragraphs is more narrowly focused on the ways in which the importance of education and the power that importance bestows have been used to institute a system of professional feudal control. These controls benefit those who run the system while depriving the American people of an efficiently operating educational system needed to promote American prosperity.

The teacher is the essential element in the educational process. All other educational personnel exist simply to facilitate the teacher-student interface. Unfortunately, the dominance of the public school system in America created educational monopolies that could control the free market for teacher's salary. These monopolies also used supply-side tactics, such as building teachers' colleges and offering free education contingent on several years teaching, to lure young men and women into the profession. Not surprisingly, this situation caused teachers' salaries to lag behind the compensation paid for similar skills in the free market. About a generation ago, teachers began to unionize to restore a competitive negotiating position between themselves and their employers. While this effort has succeeded in elevating teachers' salaries (in many cases above a free-market rate), it also institutionalized many professional feudal practices that seriously impair educational efficiency.

The seniority system discussed in the previous section is one of the primary mechanisms of professional feudalism in American education. In education, seniority is not even the number of years in the profession, but simply the number of years in a particular school district. This system seriously restricts the free flow of teaching talent to respond to changes in student enrollment patterns. In the eastern U.S., where school districts are based on counties, school district seniority is bad enough; but in California, where school districts are very local, this system is truly absurd. The issue of merit pay for teachers goes hand in hand with the issue of seniority. In a recent California election the California Teachers Association required candidates to agree with their no merit pay position as a condition for CTA endorsement. The very words "no merit pay" defy every sense of moral justice. Even many government pay systems allow for in-grade promotions on the basis of merit. I would like to believe that if the members of the California Teachers Association were allowed to vote on this issue directly, they would reject this position of their union leadership.

We need to separate the issues of seniority for employment and seniority for pay. As long as we have public educational monopolies in America, employment seniority does serve as a safeguard against union busting by school districts. However, temporary retention of employment seniority while we determine the proper structure of American education should not be used as an excuse to continue a purely seniority-based compensation system.

The teaching credential is promoted as a means to safeguard the public interest by ensuring that only qualified personnel are allowed to teach in the public schools. However, as I understand it, the teaching credential is not subject-related. Therefore, a teaching credential prevents a person who has not taken education courses from teaching; but it does not prevent a math teacher from teaching English or a history teacher from teaching physics. Many of us have had experiences such as having an English teacher teaching a computer programming course and only being one lesson ahead of the students. The ability of the system to permit such abuses makes a mockery of the safeguard of the teaching credential.

The problems of the educational system are as much caused by the industrial feudalism of the schools as they are by the professional feudalism of the teachers. Private schools function perfectly well by allowing the administration to judge the qualifications of the teaching personnel they hire without being constrained by a teaching credential. Students in private schools are free to choose which school to attend. In other words, they have a free-market choice among competing educational alternatives. If one school is overpriced for the services they provide, the private school student has the choice of taking his business elsewhere. Schools with competent teachers and administrators prosper while those who are less competent go out of business.

The voucher system is in my opinion an inspired social innovation. The voucher system offers the opportunity both to preserve the system of publicly funded education in America and to break down the existing public education monopoly that fosters industrial and professional feudalism in American education. The voucher provides for guaranteed public funding of elementary and secondary education in America, but does not require that the providers of educational services be government run. I believe that the issue of educational quality can best be served by having an accreditation program to ensure minimum standards and then letting the free market determine the results.

Each school would be required to produce an annual report presenting course offerings, educational achievements, standard test score results, teacher summaries, and other information to aid parents and students in selecting a school. To participate in the voucher program, a school would be required to accept the voucher as payment in full for all educational services. Schools would also be required to accept applicants without regard to race, creed, or color. However, they would be free to have admission standards based solely on ability.

5.19 *Recommendation: Reform feudal practices in American education.*

Institute a time-phased reform of the public educational system designed to remove both industrial and professional feudal practices. For example, we could start by instituting vouchers for public schools within school districts. At the same time, we could allow a 10 percent voucher to any accredited school, public or private. This voucher would increase by 10 percent per year to a full voucher in ten years. We could parallel this with a transition to merit pay. Starting the first year, teacher pay would be based 10 percent on merit; and this also would increase by 10 percent per year, so that after ten years pay would be completely merit-based.

I must confess that as a layman I find the furor over teacher merit pay somewhat confusing. Performance appraisals seem to work relatively well in private industry, even though the quality of your work is only well-known to a relatively few people. However, public education is a fishbowl. When I went to school and again when my children went to school, everyone knew who the better teachers were. I view public education more like professional sports, where the scrutiny of public performance makes ability differences much easier to discern. Once the voucher makes schools competitive, any administrator who fails to objectively reward his better teachers will face losing those teachers to other schools.

The Union System

The formation of employee unions was a logical attempt to restore a free-market competitive negotiating balance between a large company and its employees. A company is a political power structure formed to enhance the prosperity of its members; namely, the shareholders. Prosperity is achieved by paying the minimum amount for the inputs to production, including labor. When there is a gross size imbalance between a company acting as a unit and workers acting as individuals, the workers inevitably receive less than free-market wages. Payment of a free-market wage for workers is in the best interest of society, because suppressed wage rates both demotivate workers from doing their best and encourage the company to inefficiently utilize labor based on an artificially low value for this component of production. The extreme example of this was the military peacetime draft that resulted in college students peeling potatoes because their labor was essentially free.

Unfortunately, the competition of two large political power structures is no guarantee of a free market. In the large industrial arena when unions were weak, the workers still received less than free-market wages. However, when unions were strong—such as in the steel and automobile industries—they were able to demand considerably higher than free-market wages. While these industries controlled the U.S. domestic market for their products, such union control of wages amounted to professional feudal theft on the American public. When the steel industry was faced with foreign competition, the insistence of the steel workers union on above free-market wages resulted in the loss of many of their members' jobs to foreign companies. The U.S. automobile industry is now going through a similar crisis.

Unfortunately, the positive aspects of the union movement were eroded by several negative aspects. The strongest negative was, in many cases, the lack of responsible leadership. The problems facing union leadership are the same problems facing our national government; namely, the conflict between altruism and self-interest. Many unions fell prey to tyrannical leadership more interested in their own prosperity than in the prosperity of their members. America's failure to require the same standards of democratic control for the political power structures within American society that are required of our national government is an important cause of the feudal theft that exists in our society. Several recommendations on this subject are presented in the next section of this chapter.

The breakup of industrial trusts early in this century should have been accompanied by the breakup of industry-wide unions.

The phenomenon of a United Autoworkers Union as a labor monopoly is just as detrimental to the national interest as a single automobile company. Unions should have the same antitrust provisions applied to them as are applied to companies. This would require that each company have a separate union for its workers with no collusion on wages allowed between unions. With this arrangement there would be competition between the workers at Ford and the workers at General Motors just like there is competition between these two companies. While there would still be labor/management competition for wages, there would also be cooperation to increase their company's market share. The downsizing of American industry recommended in the previous section of this chapter will reduce the extent of industrial feudalism and will significantly reduce the size imbalance that gave rise to the American labor movement. Already the rapid growth of service industries characterized by small competitive companies has led to a natural decline in union membership.

5.20 *Recommendation: Require single-company unions.*
The social purpose of unions to restore a free-market negotiating size balance between labor and management is best served by requiring labor unions to remain within company bounds.

The rise of public sector unions is a direct threat to the democratic control of American society. Unlike private sector unions where the conflict is between two political power structures, public sector unions represent a challenge to the ultimate authority of the American people. The right of people to organize and to present their position is a fundamental right in a free society. Similarly, the right to strike against unfair management practices should also be protected. However, no group should have the right to strike against the American people.

5.21 *Recommendation: Require binding arbitration of public employee disputes by popular referendum.*

170

When public sector labor and management fail to reach an agreement on a contract, either side can request a popular referendum. Within sixty days, a popular vote will be held between the proposals of management and labor. Eligible voters shall include all those who pay for that government service. The decision of the voters shall be final. Labor and management will quickly learn that the voters will react negatively if they are called on too often to settle these disputes.

The Rise of Left-Wing Theft in American Society

The discussion of political theft in this book has been heavily weighted toward right-wing theft by the power structures that control the means of the production of wealth in society. Throughout history, right-wing theft has been the dominant form of legal theft in human society, because the ruling power structures were the only groups with the power to distort the rules of society in their favor. Left-wing groups that did not control the means of the production of wealth were (with the sole exception of the church) nonruling, and their theft was therefore illegal, or criminal, theft.

The advent of representative democracy allowed all members of society to have a more equal voice in establishing the rules of society. Representative democracy both minimized the ability of right-wing groups to legislate legalized theft and at the same time opened the door for left-wing groups to promote their own systems of legalized theft. However, when openly practiced and supported by a vigilant electorate, representative democracy is an effective barrier against all forms of legalized political theft. Unfortunately, the corruption of representative democracy in America is weakening popular control of government and strengthening special interest control of elected representatives and the functions of government. The result has been both a resurgence of right-wing theft (due to the neglect of elected representatives) and a dramatic

171

rise in left-wing theft (due to the participation of elected representatives).

While the theft by right-wing political power structures still predominates, theft by left-wing political power structures is potentially more significant. Right-wing theft involves overrewarding certain segments of the production process by distorting the free market. This distorts the allocation of resources in society and adversely affects prosperity. However, the theft by left-wing power structures, which has nothing to do with the production of wealth, is far more blatant. This blatant nature of left-wing theft makes it both more demoralizing to individual initiative and destructive to society's bond of common interest. Since left-wing theft is orchestrated through government, the battles over left-wing theft tend to paralyze government and impair efficient coordination of society. Finally, the incidence of left-wing theft (both legal and illegal) is exploding and this explosion is tearing apart the fabric of American society.

The almost continuous failure of the Democratic Party to win the presidency since the Great Society days of Lyndon Johnson is not a measure of the confidence of the American people in the leadership of the Democratic candidates. The unwillingness of the American people to elect a Democratic president reflects their fear of the groups that now control the national Democratic Party and the left-wing political theft they fear will occur if these groups controlled the presidency. Under these conditions, a perception of administrative failure by a Republican president is required for the American people to overcome their fear of left-wing theft and elect a Democratic candidate.

Government has become the primary agent of legalized left-wing theft in America and in many other Western democracies. This has occurred through the same corruption of the processes of representative government that has promoted the expansion of right-wing theft. The expansion of the federal government in the area of social welfare over the last thirty years has virtually removed the process of local popular restraint over social welfare expenditures. This reduction in popular restraint coupled with the parallel expansion of national political power structures to advocate social welfare has hopelessly tipped the balance of power in favor of government social welfare expenditures.

Government is the legitimate haven for individuals and groups seeking legal protection from theft in society. Government in an enlightened society needs to be a strong supporter of liberty and freedom from theft. However, this effect must be balanced by the recognition that the fundamental basis of left-wing theft is the same prosperity motivation that drives right-wing theft. All people wish to be prosperous and, wherever it is advantageous, they form political power structures to advocate changes in society's rules to enhance their prosperity. These political power structures always present their programs under the mantel of morality and fairness. However, their real objective is to obtain the maximum benefits for their members, not a fair return based on the value of their contributions. There is nothing surprising in this advocacy approach by political power structures. What is surprising is the ability of these groups to gain almost total control of government policy in their areas of interest.

The many nonruling groups that seek to enhance their prosperity through government action can be roughly divided into three categories: (1) lower economic groups that seek government support to reduce right-wing theft of their income and also seek left-wing theft to redistribute income and wealth in society, (2) racial or other minority groups that seek government support to reduce right-wing theft of their income caused by discrimination and also seek to enhance their prosperity by left-wing theft through preferential treatment policies, and (3) special interest groups that seek to obtain the most favorable treatment for their interest, even if that position is not supported by a majority of the American people. The following paragraphs briefly discuss each of the categories in reverse order.

Special Interest Organizations

We have become a nation of organizations. Every industry, profession, and public interest has its political power structure to present its members' point of view to society and to push for changes in society's rules to favor its members. Many of these organizations have gained near-total control over some aspect of our national life without the consent of the American people. For example, the National Rifle Association (NRA) controls gun policy, the American Medical Association (AMA) controls medical procedures, the American Bar Association (ABA) controls the legal system, the Association of Colleges and Universities (AC and U) controls amateur athletics, and so on seemingly forever. These national organizations are really political empires of professional feudalism.

The tendency of national organizations to follow extremist policies is a reflection of the advocacy mentality of their leaders and not a true reflection of the more pragmatic views of their members. One of the most dramatic examples of this phenomenon is the uncompromising opposition of the National Rifle Association to any attempts to control the distribution of guns in this country. The absolutely intolerable level of senseless violence in America is a consequence of the uncontrolled flood of firearms, not the result of a more violent streak in the American character. When responsible members of the NRA have spoken out in favor of restrictions on automatic weapons and other sensible controls, their voices have been stilled by the NRA leadership, which (I want to believe) is far more extremist than the majority of NRA members.

The first defense against political power abuse by national organizations is to ensure that they are responsive to their members and open to free expression. Like all political power structures, these national organizations can benefit American society through their specialized expertise. However, they can also use their power to steal from the American people by biasing the rules of society in their favor.

5.22 Recommendation: Foster democracy in national organizations.

All organizations would be required to permit polls of group policy paid for by the individuals wishing to conduct the poll. These polls on issues of group policy would be conducted by licensed polling companies that would poll a statistically significant random sample of the group's membership. If the poll showed more than half of the members favored a position, the governing board of the group would be required to conduct a popular vote of the entire organization. A plurality of 60 percent would establish the position as group policy and require the board to support that position.

While ensuring democratic processes within professional political power structures will help minimize extreme positions, this will not ensure that these groups act in the best interest of society. Like all political power structures, professional organizations need to be monitored by society and redirected as necessary when their policies diverge from society's interest. Therefore, the previously recommended changes to democratize government decisions and improve the responsiveness of elected representatives are also essential in curtailing the process of left-wing theft by national special interest groups.

Racial or Minority Groups

The record of human history is full of examples of the theft of income and wealth from minority groups by majority groups in society. The identifiable characteristic of these groups (e.g., race, religion, language) is sufficient to break the fragile bond of altruism that forms a common bond of humanity. The majority group often preaches racial superiority (e.g., the racial persecutions of the Third

175

Reich and the justification of slavery in America) to further dehumanize the minority group. Therefore, in a real sense, the resulting theft is predation, because the minority group is no longer considered to be human.

The modern use of discrimination to describe theft from minority groups is, I believe, unfortunate. Our use of the word "discrimination" incorrectly implies a sadistic behavior directed against another person or group. Lions do not discriminate against antelope; they prey on them for food. Similarly, human self-predation is intended by the thief as a self-directed behavior to promote his own prosperity. The hatred associated with human self-predation results from the dilemma of freedom and our emotional conflict between altruism (i.e., the brotherhood of man) and our individual opportunity for prosperity through theft. If we started calling racial discrimination theft and those who practice it thieves, we could force an honest confrontation of our feelings on this issue rather than hide behind the euphemism of discrimination.

Affirmative action and all other blanket class-based policies of preferential treatment are simply forms of left-wing theft that transfer opportunity or wealth from those who earn and deserve it to those who do not. I do not seek to deny the significant injustices that exist in our society. This book seeks to expose and then remove those injustices. However, affirmative action, which attempts to force equality of results rather than promoting freedom and the equality of opportunity that goes with it, is simply another system of injustice. Like all forms of theft, affirmative action demotivates both those receiving preferential treatment and those denied equal opportunity.

Affirmative action is potentially a very socially destructive form of political theft because it erodes the fragile sense of altruism between identifiable groups in American society. Theft by doctors or lawyers or CEOs erodes America's sense of common interest, but it does not create group antagonism because anybody could be one of these professional thieves. However, affirmative action—

whether based on race, religion, sex, or some other characteristic—creates a sense of injustice directed at the minority group in the mind of anyone who is victimized by affirmative action. If we are to preserve the altruism of American society, we must find other alternatives to promote equality of opportunity.

Remedial education programs are time-proven alternatives to affirmative action. When I was growing up, individuals who wished to attend one of the service academies, but who lacked a sufficiently strong high school background to qualify, attended a prep school to improve their academic skills. While prep school was no guarantee of college admission, those who had the inherent ability and were strongly motivated usually succeeded. There are currently many business and vocational schools in American that serve this remedial educational function.

5.23 *Recommendation: Support remedial education as an alternative to affirmative action.*
Society should both provide additional opportunities and student loans to individuals wishing to improve their educational skills to obtain employment. These programs should be strongly career-directed and carefully monitored to weed out students who fail to make satisfactory progress.

Lower Economic Groups

Poverty is simply a condition resulting from insufficient net productive effort where net productive effort is defined as gross effort minus losses from human theft or other causes. There are many factors that can cause the condition of poverty either by reducing gross output or by increasing losses. Every human society suffers from the output loss of right-wing theft that leaves middle and lower economic groups impoverished. Demotivation of effort due to misguided social systems is another important cause of poverty that affects just about every society including our own.

177

Abundance or lack of natural resources has strong correlation to national wealth. Likewise the availability of human ability enhancements through education and investment correlate strongly with national wealth. Finally, open-minded societies that promote both social and technical innovation can expect to be more prosperous.

The only way out of poverty is a job. While all the conditions discussed above influence prosperity, the fundamental requirement for material wealth is productive effort. In a free market, the distribution of income is a direct function of society's democratic assessment of the distribution of productive effort. The nonuniform distribution that results even in a free market is due to the nonuniform distribution of both motivation and ability in society.

A fundamental issue for enlightened societies is what steps should be taken to modify the nonuniform free-market distribution of income due to variations in productive effort among the members of society. The philosophical nature of this question is given additional impetus by the political power of members of society who find a free-market distribution of income to be unacceptable. These members likely include a wide cross section of society, ranging from the compassion of the more affluent members of society to the natural human envy of the less affluent members of society.

The response of an enlighted society to the nonuniform distribution of income based on free-market productivity involves two issues: (1) how much of national income should be redistributed, and (2) how should this be accomplished to minimize the adverse demotivating impacts of income redistribution. Unfortunately, any redistribution of income demotivates both those who are the recipients of additional income and those who must continue to create the income that is to be distributed.

The so-called poverty programs in America suffer from both the lack of a consensus on the magnitude of income redistribution and a lack of intelligent planning on the methods to be used. The reason for this predicament is that the redistribution of income in

178

America is not the result of a consensus between the donors and the recipients. The redistribution of income in American society is the result of a political power struggle. This power struggle pits the lower-income groups and their political allies, who receive the redistributed income, against substantial segments of the middle- and upper-income groups, who must earn and then contribute the redistributed income.

The magnitude and extent of income redistribution programs in America have gotten totally out of hand. These so-called entitlement programs now consume the largest share of the federal budget and threaten to literally bankrupt both federal, state, and local governments. In addition to supporting a wide range of lower-income groups in American society, these programs also support an ever-growing welfare bureaucracy that manages the redistribution of income to the poor and provides much of the political support for the continual expansion and misdirection of these programs. Unfortunately, this bureaucracy also absorbs a disproportionately large fraction of the funds that society intended to help the poor.

The size and extent of the income redistribution programs in America preclude any resolution by the representative process other than by actual default of the government. Only the American people as a whole through popular initiative have the power and the authority to reach a consensus on this matter that is so vital to our national survival.

5.24 *Recommendation: Establish a consensus on the percentage of national income to be redistributed as a helping-hand contribution.* The first order of business is to establish by national consensus the magnitude of income redistribution. Like a balanced budget amendment, this consensus would have the healing effect of ending the continual political battle between donors and recipients (or in many cases, victims and thieves). This would still leave the political battles over who receives how much, but the total amount would at least be agreed on.

179

A work incentive program should be instituted to completely replace the current system of income subsidy payments. Any intellectually honest assessment of poverty must conclude that below average motivation is at least as great a factor as below average ability. The present income subsidy programs flaunt this reality with the predictable result that income subsidies only further demotivate the poor from productive efforts. Political pressure from labor unions and elements of the working poor have been a major reason that America chose the income subsidy route. Welfare reduces competition for low-paying jobs by reducing the supply of low-income labor. However, as welfare rolls grow, the working poor with jobs envy those on welfare earning only slightly less. Like a black hole, welfare traps those within and its demotivating effects relentlessly pull more people in. I believe the best way to reverse this black hole of welfare is through a work incentive program. The following recommendation outlines one way such a program might work.

5.25 *Recommendation: Institute a work incentive program.*
Virtually all existing lower-income assistance programs would be replaced by a work incentive program that would subsidize the hourly wage of low-income workers. The chart in figure 5-1 illustrates how such a system might work. All Americans would compete for jobs in the labor market and workers making less than $8 per hour would receive a work incentive wage bonus. The minimum wage for employers would be reduced to $2 per hour. However, those employed at the minimum $2 wage would receive a $3 per hour helping-hand bonus paid by society for a total of $5 per hour (above the current minimum wage). This wage bonus would decrease at the rate of fifty cents for each dollar of employer-paid wages so that the bonus would fall to zero for a wage of $8 per hour.

The work incentive program would be handled for most employers through their current income tax and Federal Insurance Contributions Act (FICA) withholding program. Each employer files Form 941 returns at least monthly and most much more

HELPING-HAND WAGE INCENTIVE PROGRAM

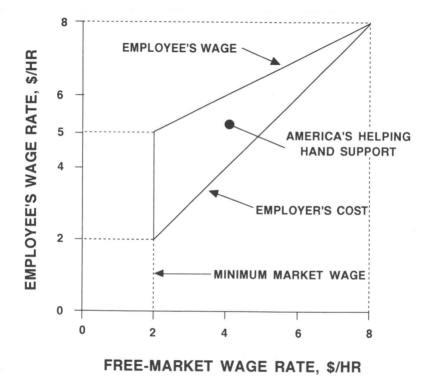

FIGURE   5-1

frequently. On the new 941, the employer would list employees' wages paid (including the wage incentive payments to low-income employees) and figure tax and FICA withholding to determine a gross tax liability. However, the new 941 would have a line for the wage incentive payments as a credit. The net tax liability would be the difference between the gross tax liability and the wage incentive payments. This would be the amount of deposit due with the return. If this amount was a credit, the bank would credit the employer's account accordingly.

While industrial, commercial, and government agencies would be substantial employers of wage incentive employees, increased employment opportunities by private individuals would be a key objective of this program. Since private citizens would be carrying a significant burden of the cost of the wage incentive program through their taxes, they should have the opportunity to benefit from its implementation. The present system discourages private citizen employers. Since the wages private citizens pay are not tax deductible, private citizens must earn $7.25 at a marginal tax rate of 40 percent so they can pay a worker minimum wage. Citizen employers also are expected to withhold FICA deductions and process W-2 forms; and for many, the threat of this paperwork alone is overwhelming.

Under the recommended program, the commercial banking system would handle all paperwork for subsidy workers employed by private citizens. Workers would open up a free account at any bank (but only one account). The bank would supply the worker with preprinted multipart forms showing his name and bank account. When the worker did work for a private citizen, the worker would have the citizen fill out and sign the form showing the days and hours worked, the agreed-on wage rate, and the total wages paid. The citizen would give the worker a check for his wages and keep a copy of the form for his records. The worker would take the check and the form to his bank for deposit. The bank would perform all the necessary payroll calculations and credit the additional incentive payment to the worker's account.

182

The recommended wage incentive program has many advantages over the present income subsidy approach to providing economic support for low-income individuals. The present system discourages work both by offering a subsistence payment for not working and by sharply reducing that payment for any income earned. The wage incentive approach only marginally discourages promotions. A worker making $2 per hour (but getting $5 per hour) might refuse a promotion to a harder job making $3 per hour (but paying $5.50 per hour), but he could not refuse to work and still receive income. Families with wage subsidy workers would be encouraged to stay together for economic reasons, compared to the present system that encourages the father to leave to allow the mother to collect welfare. This effect alone would do wonders to improve the social conditions of America's inner cities.

The wage incentive program would return to the working poor a sense of dignity and control over their own lives that is missing in the welfare state bureaucracy of our present system. A wage incentive system would help reduce the flow of low-income people to high-cost-of-living urban areas and instead encourage the flow of business opportunities to more rural lower-cost-of-living areas. Finally, a wage incentive program would allow America to find more productive employment for the many people currently employed by the welfare bureaucracy. A work incentive replacement for welfare could return America to a full-employment economy based on free-market opportunity with helping-hand assistance to those whose work is less productive than average. The economic and social boost of such a program could be a major factor in our nation's drive to reach an American renaissance.

6 / The Call to Prosperity

Whenever I visit our nation's capital, I try to schedule a visit to the Jefferson Memorial. I stand in the rotunda gazing up in awe at the words of Thomas Jefferson that encircle the dome. "On the altar of God, I swear eternal hostility against all forms of tyranny over the mind of man." Jefferson's oath is America's call to prosperity, because modern American society reeks with tyrannies over the mind of man.

America's problem is mankind's pursuit of prosperity through self-predation; namely, theft of the efforts of other men. The ideals of human liberty were clearly articulated by America's founders, and they have been rearticulated and contemporized by each generation of Americans. America's path toward an enlightened society based on those ideals has been full of temporary reversals. These reversals have been caused by wars to overcome the theft of other societies and by social redirections to overcome the theft of our own citizens. America is currently emerging from the longest war in our history. The stress of that engagement may have been partially responsible for our failure to curb the growth of political theft in American society. This threat of foreign theft and the reality of domestic theft have seriously eroded American prosperity. Fortunately, our American nation still possesses a limitless potential based on our diverse society of intelligent, innovative human beings who will respond with great motivation to an American society based on freedom.

America was founded as a representative democracy, but our present system is neither representative nor democratic. Reforms of representative government and increased popular financial support of our representatives will help improve the responsiveness of our political system. However, the power of special interest groups and the diffusion of organized single-issue voters throughout our society seriously impair the ability of the representative process to deal with crucial social issues. Democratic expression of popular will through referendums is the only way to significantly reduce the pervasive forms of both legal and illegal theft that are destroying American society.

America's two great political parties are in a very real sense vital organs of our great social structure. The Democratic Party is the heart of America. The Democratic Party embodies the feelings of compassion and mutual concern that are essential for maintaining our altruism and sense of common purpose. The Republican Party is the mind of America. The Republican Party embodies the capacity for clear pragmatic thinking and logical direction that are essential for success and therefore also essential for maintaining our altruism and sense of common purpose. The functions of these vital organs and their ability to constructively interact are being seriously disrupted by the cancer of political theft. The Republican party is weakened by the forces of right-wing theft and the Democratic Party is misdirected by the forces of left-wing theft. American prosperity requires the healthy function of both these great social organs. Only the American people have the capacity, through their democratic expression of purpose, to control the cancer of political theft in American society.

The ideals of the United States of America offer the best model for the prosperity of mankind and for all life on Earth. The wonderful diversity of humanity makes a society based on homogeneous altruism impossible. However, the light of the Statue of Liberty offers all mankind a sense of common purpose and the altruism that goes with it through individual liberty and theftless competition. The resulting self-motivated individualism provides extremely fertile ground for education, investment, and, especially, for the social

185

and technical innovations that are essential to the continued ascent of man.

America's challenge is a challenge of will, not a challenge of understanding. As we approach the twenty-first century, we need to heed this call to prosperity to carry our nation to an American renaissance. For me there are no more compelling words to express this call than the words spoken by Ronald Reagan. "If not *us, who?* If not *now, when?*" American prosperity and the prosperity of mankind await our answer.